DELIVERANCE AT SPRINGHILL PLANTATION

Eric and Cindy Davis

DEDICATION

This book is dedicated to my pastor
and the faithful members of our church
When we were under the fiercest attack from the enemy
and all seemed hopeless, obeyed the call from God
and came along side of us, covered us with fervent prayer,
surrounded us with the love of Jesus and the gifts of the Spirit, and
stood strong until the deliverance we had believed in for
so many years came to pass.

CONTENTS

ACKNOWLEDGMENTS

Jimmy and Tracy Haney

Kim and Kelly Scott

Randy and Cindy Benefield

Paulette Hickman

Christopher Hans Niels

Naomi Davis

Evelyn Adams (Photography)

And all the small group members
of our church

Introduction

Who doesn't like a good ghost story? Isn't it so intriguing to hear about old houses and the tall tales of ghosts walking the halls? I have always loved the supernatural and believed there are probably more things going on that we could not see than we could see. As I would drive by old graveyards at night, I would wonder if they could go back to the places they once lived in when they were still alive. I loved going to haunted houses in my younger years and seeing all the ghouls and goblins jumping out to scare me. Watching the old horror movies like *Dracula* and *Frankenstein* with their classic actors was something I looked forward to every Halloween. The demons and ghosts were just clean and fun, seeing as they were all make-believe anyway, and we all know nothing like this exists, correct? That thought process was what I believed in then, but now. . . not so much.

My interest in the supernatural became more real when I was around sixteen. I went to take my driver's test and passed it, but my mother was not happy. I think she was hoping I would fail so I would not be in danger of getting into an accident while driving. I can understand now, as I felt similar when my daughter passed her test. My mother would not let me drive home even after getting my printed license. When we arrived home, I told my father I had passed the test. He smiled as he gave me ten dollars and told me to drive to the store in town to get him a basketball. My mother pitched a fit, but I purchased that basketball that I knew my dad didn't need just because it gave me a chance to drive by myself for the first time.

I made it back with the basketball, and after we played for a while, it was time to get ready for bed. I left the ball in my bedroom and went to sleep. Around midnight I woke up and couldn't go back to sleep. I sat on the side of my bed. Sitting there, I saw something move in the corner of my eye and turned to see what it was. What I witnessed next took my breath away as that basketball began to roll by itself in circles. Over and over, it rolled around and even went down the hall and back again. I was frozen in terror as this event unfolded in front of me. Suddenly, the ball stopped moving. My heart was pounding out of my chest. I didn't dare to go anywhere near it. You may say this was probably a vivid dream, but I know better, as you must be asleep to be dreaming.

I wanted to tell someone about it but instead kept it to myself, figuring no one would believe me. I finally reached out to my school counselor and told her what I had witnessed that night. She listened intently during the long talk and told me she believed me. She said she thought I had a paranormal experience that night and should consider talking to my church pastor. I never did, but that experience has always been with me.

Cindy

In 1988, I met Cindy and couldn't believe she had agreed to go out with me. She was a beautiful country girl full of energy, and we enjoyed each other's company. We got married about nine months after we started dating. A few years later, our daughter Naomi arrived. As a couple, we had a unique connection: we loved history and antiques. While most couples we knew were going to the beach or the mountains for vacation, we liked going to places with old plantation homes. I always wondered in the back of my mind what it would be like for us to own one of these magnificent homes. However, with our income, there was no way we could have anything like that. So, we were content picking up a lovely antique piece for our small home that we could afford. In 1990, we had an opportunity to go back to Cindy's hometown and purchase a small home that dates to 1892. It was not a plantation home, but it was old and affordable, so we were excited to be able to get it. Now we had a wonderful home with some history and a place to begin to fill with antiques. It was our joy hunting for pieces from the 1800s. Life was good in our 1892 home.

Chapter One:
The Statue from Hell

I had to travel for my family business, and on one trip, I needed to visit some customers in the New England part of the country. In my spare time, I would look for antique shops along my way. I was in Massachusetts riding along and discovered an interesting antique shop. It was not your nice-looking, everyday place, but instead looked like a junkyard with antiques. I was intrigued, so I stopped in to browse. I looked and nothing interested me. Just when I was about to leave, someone who worked there asked if he could assist me with finding anything. I asked him if he had anything old but religious. He said he sure did and came back shortly with a family Bible that dated back to 1828. It still had things the original family had left in it. There were Sunday school lessons, newspaper clippings, and handwritten notes, all from the 1820s. I knew it was going home with me to be proudly displayed on the table in my living room. I paid just fifty dollars for it and headed out to get in my rental car. As I was leaving, the salesperson came running out and began tapping on my window. I rolled down the window, thinking he had undercharged me for the Bible and wanted more. I asked him what he wanted. He said he found something else religious and wanted me to have it. I told him I did not have any more cash to spend, but he told me he was going to give it to me for free. I thought that was odd, as who gives away stuff for free these days? He handed me a wooden statue about a foot tall. I couldn't tell what it was, but it resembled a religious figure. The problem was I didn't know what religion. I had been collecting antiques most of my life, and based on information from the shop owner as well as the type of wood the statue was carved from, I guessed it could be 150 years old or more.

Since I liked antiques, I didn't pay the origin that much attention and took the statue and thanked him. I flew home and planned to put it on my fireplace mantel. Cindy looked at it, her face showing she was not really into it, but she let it go since I had brought it back up north, and I liked it.

A few weeks passed, and we noticed some strange things. I recall sitting in my den one afternoon watching a ballgame but smelling a cigarette odor in the room. Since no one in my family smoked, I thought it must be someone outside. I walked out and around the house and could find nothing. I shrugged it off because the smell was gone when I returned. I figured it must be because the house was old, as it had weird smells and creaky floors, which was something I liked about it. It wasn't the plantation home I prayed for, but it was close enough for us at the time.

Weeks later, I saw what I thought was a shadow flash by me in the hallway, and that same smell of tobacco was in the air. The strange thing was this time it was the smell of a pipe.

More and more strange things were happening as the months passed by. We heard the steps of someone walking down the hall at night and other unexplained noises. Things were getting a bit creepy, so I decided to research the origins of our house at the courthouse. All I could find was that it was built as a sharecropper house, but the original plantation home was long gone.

After several months passed with nothing happening, we thought maybe it was just in our minds. After all, the house was over one hundred years old, so noises like this were expected. So, we decided to shift our focus to renovating the house. I loved watching the TV show *This Old House* and would get ideas on projects I wanted to do here. I continued to focus my efforts on making this old house something Cindy and I both could enjoy, not knowing that in the very near future our family would experience something so evil that our lives would never be the same.

Chapter Two:
The Small Men

It was months later, while we were fast asleep, and our daughter Naomi, who was three years old then, came into our room at about 1:00 a.m. and told us she was afraid. We asked her what was wrong, and she told us there were three small men in her room staring at her. We figured she had a bad dream, so we let her stay in our bedroom for a while until she was asleep and took her back to her room. As time passed, the noises began happening again. There were footsteps and sounds of doors closing and opening. I would see the flashes of light and shadows pass by me, and by then I was convinced this was undoubtedly not just my mind messing with me. We noticed Naomi had begun to get anxiety, and things were just not right with her. Cindy also began to experience anxiety and headaches.

We were unsure of what was going on and did not tell anyone, including the church we attended. We figured no one would believe us, and if they did, they would think we were crazy. We felt alone and nervous about the situation. Some of you reading this would say, why didn't you leave? Well, for one thing, we had just given the bank all our money on a down payment for the mortgage, and we had moved an hour away from where we were previously living. We felt we just needed to keep this to ourselves and pray to God for His help, and everything would be okay.

A couple of months later, I left to go to work as usual. While on my way, I felt the urge to pray, and something in my spirit came up about that little statue I brought home from up north. I began to have an uneasy feeling about it being in our home. All day the thoughts came back to me of how it got here and why someone would practically chase me down to give me something for free that they should be selling for a profit. Was I crazy, or could this little wooden statue have some demonic curse attached to it? Was that even possible? It was around 1995, so you couldn't Google demonic statues and get information like that. The more I thought about it, the more nervous and anxious I got.

I couldn't get it off my mind, so I decided to call Cindy from work, and I told her to take that statue out to our cattle pasture and set it on fire. It did not take her long to agree, as she did not like it anyways. She poured gas on it and burned it to ashes. I was hoping things would get back to normal now that the statue was out of our house taking with it any curse attached to it.

It was not long after all this that Naomi started to experience the men in her room again, and now the sounds of footsteps were very apparent. The smells of cigarettes and cigar smoke were happening again. I began to have panic attacks that felt like someone was sitting on my chest and I could hardly breathe. I prayed about what I could do to stop this, as I had already gotten rid of that statue. I thought, *"Have I unleashed a demonic spirit into my home, and now he has taken up residence?"*

I decided to go to the store and get a CD player to play worship music in Naomi's room at night to help her sleep. I remember getting a good CD of anointed worship music. At bedtime, we prayed over her before she went to sleep, and I started the player up. Not long after, we noticed it was not playing anymore, so I got up from the bed to see why. To my amazement, the plug was out of the socket and lying on the floor. I thought our daughter had gotten out of bed and pulled it out, but she said it was not her. I plugged it back in and went back to bed. The same thing happened an hour later, but this time I knew it was not our daughter as she had gotten in our bed, claiming the men were in her room again.

Cindy and I prayed and rebuked satan and commanded him to leave in Jesus' Name. Things began to calm down in the weeks afterward. Now maybe we could finally get some peace! Life seemed to return to normal, so we thanked God for it. We were attending church at the time, but we did not even mention this to anyone. We could imagine what would happen if this story got around in our town.

You may wonder what this has to do with a plantation home named Springhill. Well, that is all coming up, and I think you will be glad you hung around, as what you will hear is just incredible. But to tell our story, you will need to know about a few things that God set in place to make what I would say is our miracle come to pass.

A couple of years have passed, and we have not had much for the night terrors and smells of smoke. We started going to a church in Birmingham, Alabama, and were excited as they decided to add a small satellite church in our area. The church rented a building to start the new church, so after driving there to attend church for a few years, we decided to move closer to the area. After all our troubles in this house, it was not a hard decision. We called the real estate company, listed the home, and sold it shortly after. We bought a small doublewide trailer and moved it to a piece of land close to where I worked. Leaving all the chaos and depression behind and starting a new life in a new home and town was a good feeling.

Chapter Three:
The Dream

After we moved into our new home, I experienced the most vivid and terrifying dream I could ever recall. It was the kind that made your heart pump out of your chest, and afterward, there was no more sleep that night. I dreamed that my wife, daughter, and I were walking in a vast sage field, and we were holding hands together. As we were walking, I realized that we were not in Alabama. Instead, I recognized the sage grass as the plains of Africa. We were walking along, and I heard footsteps behind me and turned to see a pack of male lions approaching. Naomi screamed, let go of my hand, and took off running as two of them tracked her. Instantly I let go of Cindy's hand to go after Naomi, only to look back and witness Cindy being pursued by two of them as well. I watched in horror as they ran in opposite directions away from me, not realizing I was also being chased. I woke up having sweats and a panic attack. As the weeks passed, I constantly pondered what all this could mean, or if it was just a bad dream that I just needed to forget. The only problem was that I just could not let it go. Was God trying to warn me of something?

After the dream, my life seemed to turn for the worse. My relationships with Cindy and my daughter became strained. I always made my job the number one thing in my life, with little regard for the emotional needs of my family. After all, being a good provider was a good thing, correct? Naomi and I hardly had any relationship. She left home two weeks out of high school, and I knew why. She wanted to be away from me, and how could I blame her? When I tried to remember her childhood, I could not recall much. Cindy was experiencing anxiety and became depressed. She often mentioned how she would like to be alone and could do just fine that way. These were the loneliest days of our lives. I felt particularly isolated because of my profession. At the time, I was the associate pastor of our church. How embarrassing is it that the man who was supposed to help lead church members could not even keep his own family together? I smiled on the outside but was dead on the inside. We eventually quit the church after seeing that I had lost the anointing to pray for anyone. We did not even want to go anymore. My spiritual tank was running empty, and I had nothing to give myself, much less anyone else, including my family.

In our doublewide trailer, we did not see or hear anything as we did at the other house. All I could hear was a voice whispering that God had left me and no longer loved me due to my being a failure to my family. Even with this, I knew there just had to be a chance to seek God's face to get my family back. I just wanted an opportunity to seek forgiveness and plead for Cindy and Naomi to let me earn my way back into their lives. That dream I had sure seemed like it was more of a prophecy than just a bad dream. I knew God had warned me, and I had not listened, but I knew God was the God of second chances, and I got back into His Word and started listening to worship music, sometimes all night. Slowly, my ability to pray came back. I felt a little spiritual momentum coming about, not knowing that soon I would desperately need it.

Chapter Four:
Plantation Home Time

Even in our struggles, we both hoped for one thing—a new home. We had saved over twenty years to buy or build our dream home. The only problem was that we could never agree on a house we wanted. We went on one home tour after another with real estate agents. What I liked, Cindy would dislike, and what she wanted, I could not see us living in. We looked at homes on the lake and about anywhere we could go, but nothing appealed to us mutually. I believed that if we could find that perfect home, we would have a fresh start in our marriage. I just knew I wanted to escape from the depression I experienced in our current home. This process went on for several years without good results. My heart and mind would always return to that old plantation home with a good bit of land I had asked God for many years ago. So, with little agreement, we settled down and stopped looking for houses. Nothing in our lives seemed to make any sense anymore. I had an excellent job and a nice salary, but the money did nothing for my depression. I had a beautiful wife in Cindy, but I felt very alone. I was more like a roommate than a husband.

In the later part of 2015, Cindy and I were sitting in our den watching TV, and out of nowhere, she asked if I had seen a house in the real estate advertisements. I had given up on looking and had not even thought of houses for a while. I asked what place she was looking at, and she showed me an old plantation home for sale. As I looked, my heart almost skipped a beat. Could this be the house I had prayed for thirty years ago? Without hesitation, I agreed to look at it. It took me a few minutes to realize that it was just five minutes away from where we were living. We drove to check the place out on a cold rainy day. We pulled into the driveway, got out, and began walking around. There was nobody there, so we just started to make ourselves at home looking at everything from the outside. We did not know any history, but we could surely tell that this home was ancient and had to be from the early to middle 1800s. After a good while of looking, we both decided we wanted to call the real estate agent and ask for a tour.

I contacted the agent to request a showing, and she quickly agreed. We met there one afternoon and were super excited to go inside and check out this historic place. The agent opened the door, and it was easy to see why this house had been on the market for five years. It was filthy, and there was a real sense of depression in the air. Cindy and I were not alarmed, as we both knew the purchase of the home would be a huge undertaking. It would need to be cleaned professionally, and we had no problem with that. We continued our tour. The more we looked, the more intrigued we became. We spent more than an hour walking throughout the home. We thanked the agent for showing us the place and left.

The more we talked about the home, the more fascinated we became. We really wanted to look over the entire property without the real estate agent walking with us side by side. We were delighted that on our second tour, the realtor told us she had another home to show and left us the keys to lock up before we left. We looked at every inch of the home and property. I even crawled under the house to look at the foundation's integrity. A picture began to form in our minds of the immense history this plantation home possessed. Just from the construction, I could tell this home was different. It contained substantial hand-cut floor beams and pegs that connected many parts of the house through the wood planks. As we looked, my mind would think about the people who lived here during the 1800s. Were they like us? Did they experience the same highs and lows in life as we did? The one thing I did realize was this house was more than just an old plantation home. It was a place that seemed to have a personality of its own. With a rich history and architecture, we would soon find out how it was alive in many other ways.

I knew this was the plantation home for which I had prayed for, and Cindy agreed. We made an offer, and after some time going back and forth, we got the home. Finally, Cindy and I had the home of our dreams, and I believed a fresh start for us as a couple and family would soon begin.

I am a huge history lover. The background on the home made it a rare find indeed. The history of this property began in 1837 when a gentleman named Adam Rhinehart journeyed here from Pennsylvania and obtained the land grant. The grant was for twenty-nine acres, and he constructed a small type of cabin structure where my dining room is now. It was sold in the early 1840s and then again later that decade to a man named Heacock, a doctor from Pennsylvania. Dr. Heacock then expanded the home significantly. There were also eight slave cabins where my upper cattle pasture is now, but they no longer exist. In 1854 a smaller building was constructed next to the main home to serve as his hospital and office. He worked as the only doctor in the county during the Civil War. Historians have told me that even though there was minimal conflict here during the war, being a doctor, he would have most likely seen his share of injured soldiers. They would have come by train or horse from other areas where fighting was engaged. To my shock, the historian even said there was a good chance that soldiers were buried on this property.

I have handwritten letters from Dr. Heacock in which he wrote to his relatives back in Pennsylvania, describing his daily struggles during a challenging time in American history. He was a fervent supporter of slavery and in the letters back home to his niece, he would justify his actions by saying he treated them with integrity. His niece was very much against the practice and wrote to him voicing her concerns in several letters. The letters dated from the 1840s and ended in the 1870s. It took me about two weeks to figure out how to read these letters as the style of penmanship and how they wrote in that era were unfamiliar to me, but I finally figured it out.

It didn't take long for word to spread that we had purchased this property around the community. We knew it was dirty but could not figure out why it had been on the market for so long. I did a bit of research and found out it had been on and off the market for around five years. People claimed the house was haunted. Yet that didn't stop my interest, because I believed this was our dream home; even with the work, it was exactly what we wanted.

Chapter Five:
The Watcher in the Bedroom

We closed the property in May 2016, and Cindy and I began the necessary repairs and cleanup. As I mentioned when we toured the house, it was so filthy. We contracted a commercial cleaning company, and it took almost a month to clean the place. After the cleanup, the only thing left was to wax the floors. Cindy and I began the waxing around 7:00 pm. on a Friday. I went upstairs, and she started downstairs. The plan was to wax our way out the front door to allow the floor to dry. I was working in the back area of our master bedroom upstairs, and I felt strongly that someone or something was watching me. The feeling was overwhelming, and often I would stop and look back at the door coming into the room but see nothing and go back to my work. I began to question if this was just my mind playing tricks on me. People even claimed the house was haunted, and there were many reports of paranormal activity. I wasn't sure, but I felt uneasy and hurried to finish my work. I should have been excited to be close to moving into our dream home, but I left a little bit troubled that night.

The big day arrived, and we moved from our mobile home to the plantation. Truckload after truckload, we brought over our belongings, and the feeling of joy set in. I thanked God for hearing and answering our prayer to live in a beautiful historic place like this. The excitement of setting up our furniture how we wanted and making the home a place that we wanted was so great.

There was just so much to do in the house and outside, but finishing one project after another was a joy. The lady we purchased the house from warned us that this place was a labor of love, and the things that needed to be done would be endless. She did not know that was what attracted me to it. I could see myself in constant motion fixing floors and repairing windows and a long list of projects to accomplish, completing one project and starting another. For me it was fun, like a child at a twenty-four-acre amusement park which was all mine.

I had long forgotten about the feeling of being watched in my bedroom while waxing floors. I reasoned that it was silly to think ghosts could live here. You see all these TV shows where they look for ghosts in homes, abandoned hospitals, and prisons. I would laugh as they set up electronic equipment, and when they heard static, they believed it was the dead relative of the past speaking to them. The only dead people I would think of were those that lived here in the early 1800s. I would try to put myself in their shoes and imagine how their life compared to mine. How did the slaves that lived here feel about their lives? I would look up on that hill and could almost feel the pain they experienced living behind the house and working in the fields during the extreme heat in Alabama. I would sometimes try to imagine the sights and sounds of the occupants here. The joys and heartbreaks that undoubtedly occurred here. All the babies that were given birth in this house and the people who passed away possibly right in my bedroom. Most people might not be aware that funeral homes did not take off until the 1930s, so I knew that there were more than a few wakes that took place here, probably right in my living room. I have lived in a few houses in my life, but as I was about to find out soon, this house would reveal a secret that would turn our lives upside down forever.

My thoughts now would go back in time to when we first visited the Boone Plantation in Charleston, South Carolina, and I asked God to be able to live in a home like that. I remembered all the years of life events that brought us to this historic place. All the struggles with health issues that plagued our lives and how we fought to keep our marriage from falling apart. The mental problems that both of us endured over the years. I was overwhelmed with joy because I could now see we were here. I picture waking up in the morning and coming down the stairs to see the beautiful foyer, walking into the great room, where I knew generations of families sat and lived out their lives. I saw all the fireplaces that warmed this place during the cold winters. I could close my eyes and imagine the 179 years of Christmas celebrations here. My heart was whole as I knew things were changing for the better for Cindy and me. We would spend weekends traveling to antique stores looking for pieces that fit the period of the home. For the first time since I can remember, we were on the same page, and our relationship was good.

Chapter Six:
Fog and Night Sounds

We had been there a few months and enjoyed the new experience of owning a plantation for ourselves. I looked forward to the weekends so I could start up a new project. I had so many things to do, but they were a pleasure, not a burden. I would get up early on Saturday to start the day with a cup of coffee outside and spend a few minutes being quiet with my thoughts before getting started with the day.

One time, around 5:00 a.m., I went outside and leaned against a pole on my carport to watch the sunrise. In front of me were the barn to my right and the hospital to the left. The doctor had the hospital building built for his practice in 1854. I suddenly had a strange feeling that I could not seem to understand. The best explanation was a cold chill, even though it was a warm summer morning. What I saw next started a chain of events that changed our lives forever.

A substance that looked like fog began to roll out the barn door and slowly came across the driveway, heading toward the hospital's front door. I watched as the fog continued flowing across the yard and rolled right into the hospital's closed front door. I was trembling because I just saw something that I knew I could never unsee. No matter your beliefs, I knew this was not a good thing I had just witnessed. The feeling of pure evil overcame me as I remembered the night in our bedroom when I was waxing the floor.

The exact spot I witnessed the fog come out of the barn to the right and go into the front door of the hospital on the left.

I recalled watching some shows about paranormal things and how they walk around the house with electronic equipment, hoping to hear some static that could be the ghost of a dead relative, but this was on a new level of insanity. I gathered my thoughts and decided I needed to pray about this and try to get some revelation of what had just happened. The one thing I was sure of was that we weren't going anywhere. We had saved up money by doing without for more than twenty years and fought what seemed to be a barrier at every corner to get here. I decided this was our house, and that thing was not going to make us leave.

I have always been an analytical kind of person. When a problem arises, I go into fixer mode, usually without much forethought. That may work with issues around the house or a car that needs repair, but I was unaware of any handbook concerning what I just saw. My heart was unsure, and I knew I would need to talk to Cindy about this. She was excited about our plantation home and told everyone at work and her family how great it was. Her anxiety and depression were beginning to subside for the first time. After thinking about it for a good long time and knowing I wanted to protect my wife's heart, I decided to keep this experience to myself.

As time passed, the excitement of plantation life was so great that even though I had that terrifying experience, I hoped that maybe it was just a bad thing, and it was in the past. I was having the time of my life bringing this old house back to its original glory. Every day I noticed something I had not seen before. There were nine fireplaces, and all had beautiful hand-carved work on them. I would stand there and think how 179 years ago, a craftsman created that piece of woodwork, and I could still enjoy it in 2016. Weeks passed, and I did not feel or see anything I considered evil or dark. Hopefully, whatever that thing I saw had left the plantation.

We had been here for around six months, and life was going well. Friday came along, which is my favorite day of the week. Friday meant you could take your foot off the gas after work, and all the week's pressures seemed to dissolve. You all know what I am saying. I got off work as usual and headed home for an exciting weekend of doing the things I wanted to do around the house. I stayed busy until late and decided to get ready for bed. Cindy and I retired to our bedroom and went to sleep quickly. The cool night air and the sounds of the whippoorwills outside our bedroom window were so soothing.

At that time, we had a small Boston Terrier named Odie. He slept downstairs in the mudroom because he was getting up in his dog years and could not walk up the stairs to our bedroom. It was around 5:00 a.m., and we both woke to pots and pans clanging in our kitchen. We also heard doors opening and closing downstairs. Odie then began to bark, but his bark was different than what we were used to hearing. He had almost fear in his voice. At first, we thought maybe our daughter had come over to cook herself up some breakfast. But that was sure out of her character, as she was not a morning person.

I decided to get up and see where all the noises were coming from. I took my handgun with me, just in case. To my amazement, I eased down the stairs and found nothing was out of place. The pots and pans were still under the cabinets, and the doors were closed and locked. I checked on Odie, and he was fine. I know I wasn't just dreaming all this up, as it woke us both up simultaneously. I went back upstairs to our bedroom to see Cindy sitting up in the bed with a stunned look. She asked me what I found out, and I told her nothing was out of place, and I had no idea. What she told me next shocked me. She said while I was downstairs, a voice spoke to her in the room and said, "Hey, buddy." I asked her if that voice was in her head or if she heard that with her ears. She said it spoke out loud and very clearly.

After that morning, there was something different about the house and us. First, we began noticing quick flashes of light inside the house. It's hard to explain, but it always seemed to be in the corner of our eyesight. Then the moving shadows would dart across a room. They would move so quickly that it made us think, what was that? Also, there were cold drafts that would come past us as we were walking through the house. We were starting to be convinced that we had occupants living with us that were not of this world. I have read many stories of homes with ghosts, but none described what was happening in our home.

We began to wonder what they wanted and what their intent was. Did they want to harm us or just make us leave? This experience was not like the movie *Beetlejuice*, with sheets floating around, moaning sounds, and heads exploding. Our situation was getting more intense every week, and we had to find answers soon.

Chapter Seven:
The Gentleman Comes

It was in the fall of 2017, and like the other times, there was a break from the sounds and occurrences we had experienced. We were busy working on fixing up the house with repairs and going to antique stores to find things that interested us. The troubled thoughts had slowly eased away, and we were enjoying life now. Even the anxiety in Cindy seemed to be much better now. Cindy was spending her time arranging the house in the way she wanted. I was outside working in the yard and pasture. It took a long time for our three cats to call this place home. Our male cat, Baxter, even attempted to head back to our old house about four miles away. He was gone for about two weeks, but thankfully, he returned to settle in to make this place his home.

Cindy started a routine of feeding the cats in our barn. Every evening around sunset, she would take the canned cat food out there for them. Feeding time was their favorite time of the day, and it was so cool watching her with them in the barn built in the mid-1800s. Everything about this place could take you back to a time when life was simpler.

It was a cool fall evening, and as usual, Cindy prepared the cats' food and headed out to the barn. I was sitting in the screened-in porch. I was just minding my business looking at my phone and looked up to see Cindy in the barn, and to my horror, I saw a tall man standing just behind her. He was watching her as she fed the cats. I suddenly realized that this man was not a natural person of flesh and blood. He was dressed in a brown long-sleeved shirt and brown coveralls and wearing old worn-out boots. His attire looked like something from the 1800s. I was frozen in time as I watched the event and had no idea what to do about it. My eyes fixed on this scene, and when he looked back at me, our eyes locked on each other. Then, he suddenly vanished. For some reason that I do not understand, I gave him the name "The 1800s Gentleman." You would think I would be overwhelmed by fear, but I was not. I was more frustrated than anything seeing where this new plantation experience, I had wanted for so long was heading, and it wasn't looking good. I knew very well that the man I just saw could not have good intentions for us, but I was unsure of what to do.

I once again chose not to tell Cindy about what I had just experienced as I was very concerned about what telling her would do. She had been through so much just to get where she was, and I felt telling her would just take her mentally to a place of no return. Though I didn't tell Cindy, I found out later that my daughter did. She had a very similar experience with him when I was away taking care of my father. Below is Naomi's account, which gave me chills when she told me what happened.

NAOMI

There was one night that it was just me and my mom at home. My dad was dealing with some family issues related to his father. I was on the back porch smoking a cigarette while my mom fed the cats in the barn, about twenty yards away. I looked down for a second to put out my cigarette, and when I looked up, I saw a man standing behind my mom. He was tall and had white hair. He was wearing what appeared to be a Carhartt, long-sleeved shirt with two buttons and worn- out blue jeans. The clothes were different than what my dad described to me, but somehow, I just knew. This was the same entity. At first, I assumed that he was one of my parents' new neighbors doing something in the barn for my dad. He didn't seem harmful or to have any ill intent. I never saw his face but could see him clear as day. When my mom came back down to the porch where I was sitting, I asked her, "Who was that guy in the barn with you?" When she responded saying, "There wasn't anyone in there with me," I knew that something wasn't right. The next day, I told my dad about what had happened the night before, and the look of concern in his eyes confirmed that the trouble at Springhill Plantation was worse than I had originally believed it to be.

Eventually things calmed down after the experience, and it was like nothing ever happened. The house was peaceful with no bad vibes, and as usual, my attention would head back to doing the things we loved. We continued to go antique shopping and enjoy life here at Springhill Plantation. We didn't know that something as simple as purchasing a couch would rock our world. The sofa we brought over from our previous home was old and worn out, so we decided to buy a new one. We decided on the one we wanted and scheduled it to be delivered. The day arrived, and the truck pulled up to bring it in. We opened the door, and the two guys came in to put it in place, but we noticed how quickly they were working on getting it delivered in and out. I knew they were furniture delivery guys, but I wanted to give them a tip as it's just something I have always liked to do, so I told them to wait a minute. The look in one of the guy's eyes was of sheer terror, so I asked him what the problem was. He looked at me and said, "Don't you know this house is haunted?" I was taken aback that, yet another person was telling us this and asked him what he was talking about. He said he used to ride his motorcycle down this road, and when he would go past our house, the temperature would drop so much it would give him chill bumps. So, I asked what's so unusual about that. He replied it was happening during the summer heat, and a feeling of dread would come over him. When he found out he was making our delivery, he wanted to get out of it but knew he had to because of his job, so he just wanted to get it done and get out of there. He took off to the truck and left his tip. It may be that the Gentleman had showed himself to one of the drivers as well.

Chapter Eight:
God Help Us

It was in January 2018 that I lost my father after a battle with Parkinson's disease. I got the call around 4:30 a.m. and headed to the house to be with my mother. It was a long day dealing with grief and the things you must do when a loved one passes away. My brother and I went to the funeral home to make arrangements that afternoon, and I returned home at about 4:00 p.m. All I wanted to do was take a hot shower and rest. I first went into the kitchen to wash my hands and noticed I did not have much water pressure. I knew what was probably going on, since the temperature the night before went down to the lower teens, and a busted water line was most likely the issue. I went outside, and to my surprise, I saw water flowing out of the hospital's upper-floor windows. I rushed to turn off the water and went inside to see how bad it was. Water was pouring from the ceiling, and the lower floor was flooded. I said, "Please, God, how much more can I take today!" The only good thing was that the hospital was built in 1854, and all the wood was pure hardwood and almost waterproof. No damage besides my feelings and the water pipe behind the wall in the upstairs bathroom.

I called a contractor friend and arranged for him to come to do the repairs. He arrived around 7:00 a.m. I showed him the issue and returned to work. My neighbor was also friends with the contractor and wanted to come and help. I came home around 4:00 p.m. as they were finishing up. I went out to see the completed job, and the contractor, with my neighbor, took me outside and told me that during the day, strange things were happening inside while they were working. He said his hammer, which he had had for twenty years, went missing. I asked what was unusual about that, as I constantly lose stuff. He told me it was because he had it in his hands, sat it down, walked away for a moment, then suddenly, it was gone. They were in an area no more than four feet wide and had not moved an inch. He also said his knife also disappeared while he was using it. He said it was like something had taken it and disappeared. The carpenter said he felt like he was being watched while doing the repairs. They both were bothered and convinced that something was there with them, and they both were ready to leave. I paid him, and the thought again flooded my mind: What had we gotten ourselves into here?

Well, that was enough for me, and it was time to seek help from the spiritual side. We had not attended church for years and did not have what you would call a church family or anybody I could confide in coming along to our side to help. I went and spoke to a couple of people who were Christians and found out quickly that when it comes to ghosts, if that's what you want to call them, most people will head to the hills. It's intriguing to read about them and watch TV shows in the comfort and safety of your home, but to come over to my house with the possibility of running into one was not going to happen with the Christians I knew. Now I began to realize that this battle was going to be a one-on-one fight, and Cindy and I would be the ones who would be taking this battle on alone. I started looking to the Scriptures to seek the stories of encounters with demonic beings. I was raised in the church but could not recall any sermons or teachings about what we were experiencing here at the Springhill Plantation. The only one I could remember was a preacher who came to our church and was active in the satanic movement back in the 1970s, but that didn't help as we were not involved in anything that I knew of that would invite them into our lives. I started in the New Testament and was amazed at how many stories there were on the subject. I read the books of Matthew through Revelation and saw just how common it was for people to be oppressed and possessed by demons. I have prayed against the power of satan for years, and it wasn't like I hadn't heard or was ignorant of demons, but what was happening here was different than anything I had read or even watched on TV. I had heard of encounters on some of these shows where they brought in electronic equipment to attempt to get some response from the spirit. I did not need anything like that, as I had just seen one of them right in front of me, and it was aware that I saw. Cindy's mental and physical health was declining rapidly; she seemed to be the target for most of the attacks, so I decided it was time to rid this place of their presence.

Chapter Nine:
The Anointing Oil

And they cast out many demons, and anointed with oil many who were sick, and healed them.

Mark 6:13

I read in Mark 6:13 about how the disciples drove out demons and used anointing oil in their ministry, so I decided that if it worked for them, it would work for us. I had a friend traveling to the holy land, and I asked him to get me some anointing oil and bring it back with him. He agreed, and about two weeks later, after he returned, he gave it to me. I was familiar with this type of oil as I had seen it used in our church when we attended years earlier. I asked Cindy if we could pray over each other and anoint the house, and she quickly agreed. She knew that many of her mental health issues were partly due to the oppression she felt after we moved here. One of the most important things I learned in church was that we have three parts. We are a spirit; we have a soul; and we live in a body. If we neglect any of these three, we can invite many troubles into our lives, and I knew we had at least neglected the spirit realm. We tried to take good care of our physical and mental health. Cindy had seen several doctors, was taking medication to help with several conditions, and had reasonably good results. We knew these health issues, especially the mental side, were getting out of control after we moved here.

Cindy and I gathered in our den with the anointing oil, and after placing the oil on our foreheads, we got up and started walking through the house praying. We would put the oil on the doorframes all over the place. I didn't realize just how many doors we had here. Cindy was following me in reading Psalms 91 from the Old Testament.

He who dwells in the secret place of the Most High
Shall abide under the shadow of the Almighty.
I will say of the LORD, "He is my refuge and my fortress;
My God, in Him I will trust."

Surely He shall deliver you from the snare of the fowler
And from the perilous pestilence.
He shall cover you with His feathers,
And under His wings you shall take refuge;
His truth shall be your shield and buckler.
You shall not be afraid of the terror by night,
Nor of the arrow that flies by day,
Nor of the pestilence that walks in darkness,
Nor of the destruction that lays waste at noonday.

A thousand may fall at your side,
And ten thousand at your right hand;
But it shall not come near you.
Only with your eyes shall you look,

And see the reward of the wicked.

Because you have made the LORD, who is my refuge,
Even the Most High, your dwelling place,
No evil shall befall you,
Nor shall any plague come near your dwelling;
For He shall give His angels charge over you,
To keep you in all your ways.
In their hands they shall bear you up,
Lest you dash your foot against a stone.
You shall tread upon the lion and the cobra,
The young lion and the serpent you shall trample underfoot.

"Because he has set his love upon Me, therefore I will
deliver him;
I will set him on high, because he has known My name.
He shall call upon Me, and I will answer him;
I will be with him in trouble;
I will deliver him and honor him.
With long life I will satisfy him,
And show him My salvation."

Psalm 91:1–16

As we moved from room to room, an extraordinary feeling of pressure began to surround us, which was hard to explain. A sense of resistance may be a better word, but we both knew that we had stepped into something from which there would be no going back. The stronger the opposition, the louder I would pray and rebuke the demons. I was repeatedly shouting the name of Jesus and commanding them to flee this house. God reminded me that the power in us was more than them and not to back down. It was nothing like the movie *The Exorcist*, but there was a tangible electric feeling of a spiritual battle going on over us.

We continued throughout the house and headed to the doctor's office/hospital built in 1854. If you remember, that was where the fog I saw went when we first moved into the house. We opened the door with anointing oil in hand and continued our battle. It was a whole different ball game over there. The pressure and resistance were mighty, but I knew I could not let even a little fear overtake me. Now I knew why nobody wanted to go into that house. It had a feel to it that caused anxiety. I always wondered what I would have seen in that place if I could return to the Civil War time. The sickness, wounded soldiers, and, of course, death. Could these spirits have anything to do with that time in history? I did not know, but they could not stay with us no matter what. We continued to pray, confessing the name of Jesus and reading Psalm 91.

Then a rush of power came through the place so much that it made chill bumps form on me, and after that, a wonderful sense of peace set in. I knew it was over, and the spirits had left. We were covered in sweat and tired, but it was a good kind of tiredness. We went back into the main house, and I looked up at the clock and realized we had been praying for over two hours. We both got ready for bed and slept the most peaceful sleep we'd had in a long time. I was glad this was a Friday, and I had the weekend off. We were so thankful to God for delivering us from the spirits. We also did not tell anyone what had happened. My mind said that if we did, everyone would call us crazy. But that wasn't important, as we did not have anyone we trusted enough to tell anyway.

Years of anointing oil buildup on our doorframe.

Chapter Ten:
Haint Blue Ceilings
and Hell Breaking Loose

During the months to follow, occasionally, we would have neighbors stop by to chat, and without fail, someone would say, "I heard this house was haunted?" Even one older gentleman said, "Hey, have you seen any of them haints?" I had to ask him what he meant as I was not privy to what a haint was.

He explained that a haint was a ghost that would chase you around the house until you were exhausted and sometimes sit on your chest at night to suck out all your energy. If that was not terrifying enough, He then showed me the color of the ceilings on all my front porches. He said it's called haint blue which is supposed to ward off evil spirits because they hate the color blue that looks like water. Apparently, these types of ghosts didn't like getting close to water. I was alarmed as I was now thinking the haint blue ceilings could be blocking their way out of the house, but I was also skeptical that an evil spirit would not pass by a particular color of paint mixed at the local hardware store. After researching the reasons for the practice, I found out enslaved African Americans initially used it to combat haints or evil spirits that escaped their human forms at night to paralyze and injure the occupants of the home. They used dye produced at low country indigo plantations to make the paint. I now wondered why it was painted on my ceilings and how long it had been there. Could the porch ceilings being painted haint blue be a message of something wicked that we had missed? This house was beginning to reveal secrets of its past. What other things did we not know about this place? Who else has seen our visitors in the past? Could these secrets be the reason the past owners may not have stayed very long? In the beginning when people would say, "You just bought a haunted house," I would just chuckle. However, after the many experiences that we encountered in that house, that chuckle from once before became a chill in my soul.

After the man left, I heard that evil familiar voice whispering, "You know why the ceilings are haint blue, don't you?" Bothered, I began to consider calling a painter to change the color to something else. Instead, I prayed and felt in my spirit that God was telling me not to obey the voices I heard. In my heart I believed that God moved us to this plantation home to make it ours the day I prayed for one, twenty-nine years ago, after touring the Boone plantation in South Carolina.

Haint Blue Ceiling on my front porch

Months passed, and again we returned to our happy place of shopping for antiques and doing the things outside we loved to do. Our place was beginning to shine so much we were having cars stop in front, and people would get out, taking pictures. You may wonder how, after repeated hellish experiences, we could go about our everyday lives afterward. That is something we can't fully answer, but we now believe we were slowly getting conditioned by demonic forces to accept them and give in. They knew we had put everything we had to get to this place, and just packing up and moving was not going to happen easily. They had time on their side and could have been here for over 180 years. We know that sometimes in life, you think you know what you would do in a bad situation, but life looks different than theory, and what you thought is not necessarily what you would do.

Many months later, after the night we anointed the house, there was still a sense of peace in the home. We were going about our lives of working at our jobs and enjoying life on Springhill Plantation. I remember it was a Friday morning when I woke up at 5:00 a.m. and went downstairs to begin my day as usual. I prepared my coffee and sat down on the couch. Suddenly a feeling came over me that I could not fight off, and that feeling was an overwhelming hatred for Cindy. There was no good reason for this feeling as we were getting along just fine, and for the first time in a long time, our lives seemed to be in a good place. I tried to fight these thoughts off, but they would not let up. My mind was racing, and my heart was beating out of my chest. I thought of how much I would like to be rid of her. Honestly, I couldn't have cared less if she was dead, and the thought of her made me sick. I got up and went to work, knowing she would be there soon to do her job at our plant. I tried to pray it away, but nothing I was doing could make the thoughts disappear.

She arrived at work happy as ever, but I could not even look at her, and when she approached me to ask a question, I would walk away. The feeling of rage did not let up all day to the point I was getting physically sick. I don't believe a Christian can be possessed, but this was getting close. I managed to avoid her all day, but as the workday was about to end, Cindy came up to me and asked if I could take her to a local antique store. I reluctantly said yes, and we got in my truck and headed out. I did not speak a word during the trip, and when we arrived, I got out and went into the store alone. The entire time I never let myself get within her speaking distance. I didn't know she had called our daughter and told her what was happening. I believe God has given my daughter the ability to read my mind, so I have never been able to hide my feelings from her. She told Cindy she was going to the house as fast as possible.

We arrived home, and Naomi drove up and immediately took me outside to talk. She looked into my eyes, told me she loved me and asked me what was wrong. I wept uncontrollably and told her I did not know what was happening and why I felt that way. She held me in her arms and said we would work this out as a family. She went in to talk to Cindy as I stayed outside. Shortly she came back out and told me what she wanted to do.

She told me she was going home to get some sage she had purchased, and we would burn it inside the house. I didn't know anything about sage, but she explained that for centuries it was used to help drive out harmful spirits. I knew there was no power in the smoke itself but only the blood of Jesus, but I did not care if it helped in the situation, we were in.

She left to get the sage, and another feeling began to overwhelm me while she was gone. It was not the sense of hate for Cindy that had overtaken me all day, but a rage aimed at whom I now knew were to blame. The spirits were back, but this time they did not appear to me like before but were attacking my mind with these terrible thoughts. I began to pray and felt in my spirit to get out the anointing oil and pray over the house as we had many months ago but also to allow my daughter to use the sage as she asked. She drove back up, and I told her what I felt we should do, and she quickly agreed. We gathered outside to pray together and lit the sage to begin the house cleansing.

What happened next is an experience I shall never forget. With the sage lit and smoke flowing hard, we entered the house, but I felt more than a resistance this time. They wanted our home and, I believe, also our lives. But, unlike last time, I possessed a wave of holy anger that drove me to speak directly to them, commanding them to leave this house. I pleaded the blood of Jesus over us and shouted God's praises at the top of my lungs. I was screaming out the name of Jesus as we walked through the home. The house was filling with the smoke of the sage, and it was getting difficult to see.

When we anointed and smoked the entire downstairs, we headed up to the second floor, where I had seen most of the light flashes and moving shadows in the earlier days. As we headed up the stairs with the sage burning hot in Naomi's hand, but something kept blowing out the sage.

Undeterred we relit the sage again and continued ahead. The top of the second-floor stairs had always given me the creeps, so we put in a framed picture of Jesus up there. As we approached the small door that allowed access to the attic, I sensed something evil behind that door. I opened that door without fear, and my daughter reached in with the sage. I stuck my head into the attic and shouted at them to get out in the name of Jesus! What I heard next almost freaked me out. I heard a scream come from the back of the attic, and nobody heard it but me. However, it did not scare me. Instead, it motivated me more in the spirit to pray harder.

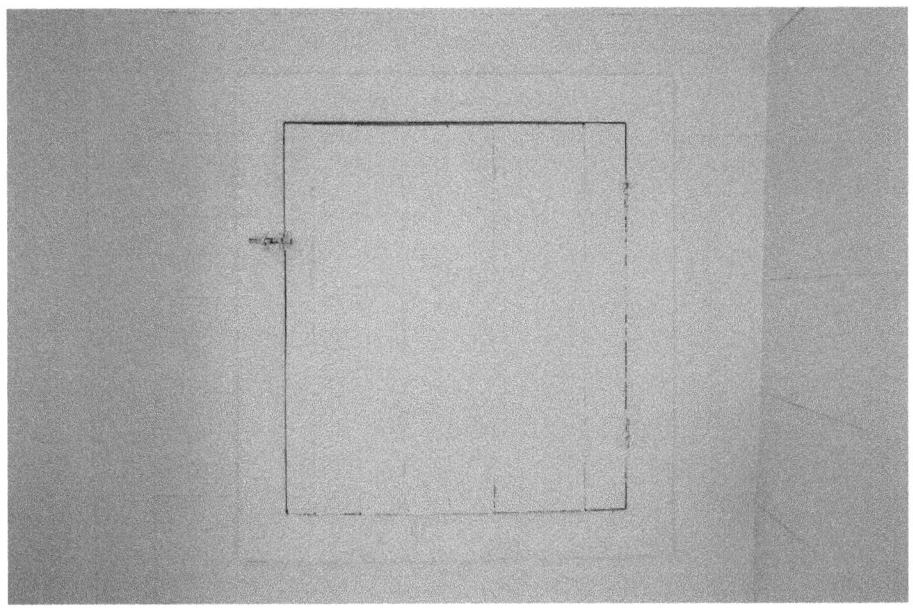

The attic door where I heard the screams.

I had prayed for God to send angels before we even started, and I could very much sense their presence at the top of the stairs. With the power of God increasing, we continued to the hospital to take the battle to them. I knew in my spirit that we were about to see the worst when we got there.

There was a door in the bottom staircase that you could use for storage, and as I stood in front of it, I felt the pressure of something behind it. I flung the door open, and my daughter filled it with smoke after I commanded them to leave in the name of Jesus. I heard the sounds of barking dogs coming from the back of the storage area. There was a heightened sense of knowing there was a battle between good and evil, and the evil side was getting beaten down hard. It felt like a heavyweight fight for the ages. After going upstairs with the smoke and prayer, it was over, and I knew they had left. We were all covered with sweat and the smell of smoke.

I know now that the sage had no power or effect on what happened that night, but I was under an immense attack that day and was desperate for answers. My daughter chose to use sage to go into battle with these demonic spirits. Was there a connection to the sage field I saw during that dream? Was God showing me a sign of things to come? I cannot answer that, but I was so grateful to my daughter for taking the lead when I was under the most intense attack and at the weakest point in my life. She could have probably done like many people I know and fled, but without fear she decided to take the fight directly to them to defend her family.

Exhausted, we returned to the main plantation home to

open all the doors and windows to let the sage smoke out. I was glad nobody drove past this house as I knew they would think it was on fire and call the fire department. I was so grateful to God for His anointing and for sending His holy angels to fight this battle on our behalf.

Knowing what I know now, I may not have used sage. However, at that moment, it appeared the best option. It is easy for us to connect with outside options when everything we have previously tried does not work. One thing I encourage every believer to know and fully understand is the only prevailing authority is the authority of Christ. He has given us everything we need in Him for life and godliness, and we don't need to look outside of Him for freedom, breakthrough, or deliverance. I am thankful for God allowing this experience to be a part of my journey because it showed me even more how He is the answer to every problem.

Chapter Eleven:
A Growl in the Woods
and the Voice in the Dark

Then he said to me, "Do not fear, Daniel, for from the first day that you set your heart to understand, and to humble yourself before your God, your words were heard; and I have come because of your words. But the prince of the kingdom of Persia withstood me twenty-one days; and behold, Michael, one of the chief princes, came to help me, for I had been left alone there with the kings of Persia. Now I have come to make you understand what will happen to your people in the latter days, for the vision refers to many days yet to come."

Daniel 10:12–14

I wanted to talk to someone about this and remembered someone out of state I knew was in the ministry. I called him but was reluctant to mention what was happening after talking to others. Finally, I did strike up a conversation about demonic spirits inhabiting our home. He was attentive and listened to our story. After I told him about the multiple episodes of encountering these spirits, He asked me if I was familiar with territorial spirits, and I told him no. He said Daniel chapter 10 speaks of it. Daniel received a troubling vision and prayed to God. In response, God sent the angel Michael to come to Daniel to interpret the vision. Michael encountered the prince of Persia, and the evil spirit fought him for twenty-one days. I asked what that meant to me, and he said that just as there was a demonic spirit in charge of the country of Persia, one could very well be attached to our home. I told him we had anointed our home numerous times. He responded, "Have you anointed your property?" I was unsure what that meant, and he told me it was time to go to the four corners of our property lines to do as we had done inside the house. He could not be sure but said it was possible that when we prayed over our house, they left but were not far away and waited until we became weak in spirit and made their way back to us inside the house. I thanked him for the information and concluded the call.

Intrigued about what he told me, I prepared my heart with prayer and headed to the corners of my property to do just that. I took a small handheld chain saw with me, and I intended to cut a cross sign into a tree at each property line and place anointing oil inside the cuts. For some, I know this must sound like I was beginning to lose my mind, but I was so ready to live a simple peaceful life that I was prepared to do anything to achieve it.

One of the trees I cut the sign of the cross into on my property.

One of my property lines was on the top of the mountain, and I found a tree near the corner. I cut the shape of a cross, anointed it while praying in the Spirit, and moved on to the next. I could feel the presence of God as I moved from one corner to the next, and by the time I got to the last one, darkness was falling. I found a small pine tree to cut the final cross into, and as I applied the oil in the dark, I heard the distinct sound of a growl back further into the woods. Not afraid, as I already listened to this before inside the house, I shouted the name of Jesus into the darkness and proclaimed that no weapon formed against me would prosper. I once again kept this event to myself and said nothing to Cindy about it.

The cross cut in the small pine tree where I heard the growl in the woods.

I got back to working on different projects around the plantation, and I wanted to remove a barbed wire fence and replace it with a wood fence made from rough-cut lumber. The thought was to create it to look like it was from the 1800s. I knew just who I wanted to come to build it. We had met a young couple in the cattle business, and he also built wooden fences for a living. We had kept in touch since 2014 when we were together in Rome, Georgia, doing marriage counseling. I called him to ask if he was interested, and he said he would love to come. We planned for when he would come, and he asked me if a hotel was nearby. I told him he was welcome to stay here because I knew building this fence would take a couple of weeks. The hospital building had been remodeled inside into a guest house and would be perfect for him. We have called that hospital the "Little House" since we moved here.

It had been a good long time since we had heard or even felt anything evil like we had previously. I will never forget what happened that night, but I did not dwell on it much anymore and was grateful that it was in the past. I called Chris when the time was close for him to come, and we talked about some of the stories we had experienced while living here.

I had called Chris several times when we felt something terrible was going on to pray for us. Chris was now a strong Christian who had traveled the world seeking other religions when he was younger. I felt I needed to warn him about the Little House as nobody had ever slept over there since we had been there. Even my daughter didn't want to go over there. Once she swore, she saw a face in the window one night as she drove to see us. He told me he had no issue at all, and if something were in there, it would just have to leave while he was staying.

He arrived around 10:30 p.m., and I helped him move his bags inside. I showed him everything he may need and said good night to head back to go to bed. I told him we would meet the following day at 9:00 a.m. to discuss my plans for the fence building. I went to bed to retire for the night and got up and went to work after a good sleep.

The following day I came back to make plans with Chris, but he said he wanted to talk first. I asked him what was going on. He said he had a wild experience early in the morning in the Little House. Curious, I asked him what happened. Here is how he explains it.

CHRIS

In the summer of 2019, I was invited by Eric to stay on his plantation for a few days and help construct a fence for his cattle. He had shared stories of his eerie encounters on the property, but I was skeptical. I was to stay in the guest house which was originally a hospital during the war.

My first night, I slept well but was awakened around 4:00 a.m. I almost instantly heard an audible voice say,

"Are you awake yet?" My rational mind thought Eric must have been up early and wanted to get started working. I looked out the window toward his home. It was pitch black. Immediately, I knew I was the only person in the home. Somewhat frightened, I also felt tired and a little sick. I rolled back over, closed my eyes and vowed to deal with whatever it was in the morning. The following day I prayed over the home and my stay there and never had another encounter again.

I was glad Chris could take his authority to drive it away, but the realization that the spirits were still here even after all we had been through and done began to weigh heavily on my mind. Not only had they given us all kinds of trouble, but now they were audibly speaking to a guest of mine. He had no more issues the rest of his time here and, after three weeks, finished the fence. I was so appreciative of Chris for not leaving the instant that voice spoke to him in the dark.

Chapter Twelve:
Life Is Different This Time

After Chris left, things seemed different than they had been before. I would not allow myself to go to that happy place I would typically go to after having a bad experience and praying for deliverance. I now kept up my guard and reacted to anything that felt not ordinary. A bump or noise in the house would trigger me to rebuke the devil and get the anointing oil to apply all over the place. We both questioned any feelings we had that we felt were negative. I knew the devil was not responsible for everything that was not right in my life, but I could not get over the thoughts. There was a hopelessness that slowly began to overtake me. It was not something that happened quickly but was drawn out over almost a year. I would pray, but it seemed to be ineffective. I could tell something terrible was happening, but I could not figure out why. *Did we not just drive the spirits out a year ago?* my mind would say. *What could we have done to open doors and allow them back?* I searched my heart for anything we had done, but I could think of nothing.

We have never dabbled in the occult, and we tried to live as good Christians. The last time I could recall that I had participated in anything like that was when I was eighteen.

A couple of friends and I got a Ouija board and began playing with it. Like teenagers, we asked silly questions like if this girl liked us, etc. It was my turn, so I wondered what my future wife's name would be. I asked, and as we moved the handpiece around the board, something took over, and by itself, it spelled out the name Heidi. That was terrifying enough that we packed up, left, and swore never to play that game again. That weekend we decided to watch a high school football game out of town. We were hanging around the fence next to the field observing the game, and up came this blond-haired girl who said to me, "Hello, what's your name?" It took me back somewhat as cute girls like that have never approached me like that. I told her my name was Eric and asked her what hers was. She smiled and responded her name was Heidi. Me and my friends just stood there silently and could not believe what she just said. Who was she and how did she know to come to us? That was officially the last time I messed around with the occult. Anyway, the devil is still a liar. As you all know, my sweet wife's name is Cindy!

We were not perfect, but one can ask, what did we do to deserve this hell on earth? I noticed Cindy was drawing back from me and dealing with her health issues. She was sleeping all the time, and her headaches were returning. I had seen nothing and heard nothing like last time, but my heart was growing heavy.

I dealt with depression on and off all my life, and my coping mechanism would be to do yard work, so that's what

I was doing most of the time. While cutting the grass and working in the pasture, I found myself going over in my mind all the events that happened in the last few years. Like a tape recorder, they would rewind, replay, and repeat. The one thought was, what was I missing? We had no friends to lean on, so we stayed here all alone at the Springhill Plantation. The very place I had fought so hard to be able to receive was now becoming our prison. We found ourselves living separate lives again with TV as our closest friend.

My health also began to have issues as panic attacks and insomnia became more frequent. I watched Cindy recluse herself deeper into the darkness. Cindy, on occasions, would reach out for me to pray for her, and I would lay hands on her to pray, and things would be better, but it just lasted for a little while. She had gotten to a point where she didn't even want to go and get the mail from outside. Our daughter told me she believed her mom had a social disorder called agoraphobia. It was the fear of leaving our house and being around other people or crowded places. Even though I knew what was happening I didn't have the energy or spiritual motivation to fight back.

It was the late winter of 2020, and our lives were still not going very well. I had gone to work, and sometime around lunchtime, I became bothered in my spirit and went back home to check on Cindy. I arrived and went upstairs to find her almost unresponsive and very sick. Cindy was talking but making no sense at all. I was a former paramedic in the military, so I immediately began to check her for signs of a stroke. I did the tests but did not believe that was the problem, so I called our daughter to come over to help me get Cindy downstairs so we could get to the emergency room. We arrived at the hospital, and they began doing all sorts of tests to see what was wrong. They did a CAT scan and multiple blood tests. Afterward, the doctor came in and said they could not find anything wrong with her. They checked her drug list and said they thought two of the meds she was taking might be causing this, but they were unsure and sent her home. With no good answers from the doctors, I only became more depressed about all that was going on. We went back to our dark home and lonely lives. I was supposed to be the spiritual leader of my family, but I now felt powerless.

Chapter Thirteen: Mad Enough to Fight!

Therefore submit to God. Resist the devil and he will flee from you.

James 4:7

The spring of 2021 came, and we were still moving along with no purpose or plans for our lives. One night during the week, I went upstairs to get ready for bed, and Cindy was in the shower. I was standing next to our bed doing exercises for my feet that I have struggled with for years. Our daughter's dog, Zoe, stayed with us while she was attending college. As I was busy doing exercises, Zoe suddenly stood up on our bed and began to growl fiercely. I turned around and saw a tall black figure with no face pass through the wall from my bedroom and go toward the bathroom where Cindy was taking her shower. I can describe it as over six-feet tall with a very dark, transparent foggy appearance. It had long flowing sleeves, but I could see no hands. The demon had no eyes, but I knew it was looking at me. I could see no feet as it levitated off the floor. The evil that permeated from it was overwhelming. The closest thing I can think of would be the look of the grim reaper I had seen in horror stories. Zoe leaped off the bed screaming, running downstairs as fast as she could. Rage came over me at the thought of it trying to harm my loved ones. I knew I had just seen a high-ranking spirit sent from satan to destroy us, and so did Zoe. He was the one sent from satan just for us and, I believe, the leader of the rest of them that dwelled here.

I went into battle mode, praying in the Spirit and rebuking the devil in Jesus's name. I reacted instantly and pursued it out of the room as an intruder that had come to harm Cindy. My weapon was the name of Jesus and the power of the Holy Ghost in me. It was over as soon as it happened. I do not know where it went, but it had left the house the instant I spoke the name of Jesus. I had to sit down and calm myself after it happened. I did not have the heart to tell Cindy, as I knew she would be unable to take it in her mental state. I took our anointing oil and put it all over her pillow that night. It was a restless night of troubled thoughts, wondering why God would allow us to go through this for so long and all alone. The following day after I came home, she asked what was on her pillow, and I told her a white lie. I said I was praying for her before I went to bed and used some anointing oil but did not mention what I encountered in our bedroom.

A couple more months passed, and I had no more sightings, but I knew they were still hanging around. The oppression was getting stronger as the weeks passed, and I hated my life more and more. I was starting to lose hope that this nightmare would ever end. The Springhill Plantation was now alive with a heaviness that seemed endless.

Zoe

Chapter Fourteen:
The Last Straw

How long, LORD? Will you forget me forever?
How long will you hide your face from me?
How long will I store up anxious concerns within me,
agony in my mind every day?
How long will my enemy dominate me?

Consider me and answer, LORD my God.
Restore brightness to my eyes;
otherwise, I will sleep in death.
My enemy will say, "I have triumphed over him,"
and my foes will rejoice because I am shaken.

But I have trusted in your faithful love;
my heart will rejoice in your deliverance.
I will sing to the LORD
because he has treated me generously.

Psalm 13:1–6 CSB

In May of 2021, I got up around 4:30 a.m. to prepare for work and headed downstairs. I got my coffee and sat on the couch, trying to wake up. Most mornings, I would attempt to pray as best as possible, but today it was a struggle to get any words out, so I sat in silence. Our den, where the TV is, joins our entrance foyer that leads upstairs to the second floor. I was sitting in silence when a loud voice behind me in the foyer shouted out my first name, and I instantly knew the voice was not human. It was so loud that it rocked the house and caused me to go into a panic. I was so shaken that I almost spilled my coffee. They had appeared in front of me before, but now they were talking to me out loud. That was a new twist in this harrowing story that would never seem to end.

The foyer where the voice shouted out my name.

When something like this happened, my usual response would be fervent prayer and anointing of oil, but this morning I did nothing. I had nothing in my spiritual tank to fight back with and no weapon of warfare I felt worthy of calling on. So, I just continued sitting on the couch, shaken up. The evil spirits were officially living here with us and making themselves at home. We had at least two of them because I saw them on different occasions, but I suspect there were many more that I was not allowed to see.

It was a couple months before I saw them clearly again, but the oppression never ceased. When July came, I had descended into a place of losing all hope that anything would ever change, and feeling this would be our destination of misery. I tried to keep myself busy at work and with endless chores. If I could think of anything that needed fixing, I was all over it with a passion. The busyness would keep my mind off what I thought the truth was—that my life would never change. Insomnia had become a real problem, to the point that I was taking Ambien and a mixture of over-the-counter sleeping pills to get through the night. Even in this mental state, I still was trying to pray daily for God to please come to help us out of this situation.

I went to work as usual on a Thursday. It was a busy day, and I was looking forward to coming home to start a new project on the farm. I drove up around 2:30 that afternoon and parked my truck in the carport. I got out to head into the house, and that familiar feeling overwhelmed me. I knew something was horribly wrong, and I looked up toward the window where Cindy's office was. There he was, standing in her window, looking down at me. The same spirit I had named "The 1800s Gentleman" that stood over Cindy in the barn years ago was looking down at me. He did not move, and we locked eyes with each other. It went on for over a minute, and as he folded his arms, he faded out of sight. I went into a panic attack and struggled to breathe in his presence. The evil permeating from him was more than I could stand, and I turned and walked away. My mind was screaming with thoughts of hopelessness and despair. I took some time and eventually went back into the house to find Cindy at her desk working. He was standing within six feet of her the whole time.

Office window where I witnessed the 1800s Gentleman.

There was no way that I was going to tell Cindy what happened. That night I went outside, knowing I had taken all that I could stand. I walked up to the front of the hospital house and looked up at the night sky that was filled with shining stars. I then completely broke down in tears over all the years of troubles we had experienced here. Then, in a rage, I looked up to the night sky and screamed as loud as I could these words. "GOD, WHERE ARE YOU?" I looked up again and said, "GOD, PLEASE HELP US!" The tears were flowing uncontrollably at this point. After a few minutes, I calmed down, and a feeling of peace began to come over me and a nudge from the Spirit to be quiet. I stood in silence for a while, and then a single word came into my spirit, and all I heard was the one-word name of a local church in our area. It did not make sense at that moment, but shortly, it came to me, and I knew what it meant.

Chapter Fifteen: Calling the Calvary

And if one member suffers, all the members suffer with it; or if one member is honored, all the members rejoice with it.

1 Corinthians 12:26

I went on to work the next day with a renewed hope that maybe something was about to happen. I was grateful I had received the word from the Lord the night before, and I knew of the church I had heard in my spirit as it was just south of us, about twenty minutes. I had passed by that place hundreds of times, visiting customers and shopping, etc., and I also knew someone close to me that attended. We had not been to church for years and did not even want to go. The busyness of my work and everything Cindy and I had been through made us too tired to even think of getting up on a Sunday morning. I had too many projects to do, and I knew Cindy wouldn't be able to wake up that early anyway. Sunday was a day to get stuff done and rest. After all God called it the day of rest, didn't He?

All day my mind tugged at me to give a call to Tracy, who I knew attended that church. I had seen her at Walmart a few years back, and she mentioned that's where she and her husband were going, and they loved it. I tried calling several times during the day, but my fingers would not let me press her phone number. There was such resistance to contacting her. My mind was saying, "*If you ever tell anyone what you are going through, they will say you are deranged*". There was even a voice in my head trying to convince me that I had made the whole thing up, but I knew that was an absolute lie.

I decided the first thing I would do was to send her a simple text asking her if she still attended. That way, if she responded no, I was in the clear before calling her and making a fool of myself. I quickly got a text back that said yes, and are you thinking of visiting? I gave it a few days and then decided to give her a call.

I made the call after I got home from work, and after a little bit of small talk, we began to talk about church. I was nervous, but I went ahead and pushed through my anxiety to ask her if the church she attended had any dealings with demonic spirits. To my surprise, she said yes and even mentioned someone who was a leader in that part of the church's ministry. I began to tell her the stories of our troubles at the Springhill Plantation. She invited us to come on Sunday, but even I knew that was going to be easier said than done. We have not been to church in many years, and we both had become accustomed to Sundays as a day of rest. Getting Cindy to go with her sleeping issues would be challenging, even if I wanted to go. Mornings were just hard for her to get up and get going. After a good chat, Tracy said she would have the small group she was attending pray for us.

I was aware of the word that I believed God spoke to me that night, but I was also extremely nervous to approach Cindy to inquire about the possibility of attending a church service again. In the last few years, we stopped attending church due to the mounting health and mental issues we were experiencing. It may not have been what we should have done, but it sure was easier to be a stay-at-home Christian. I knew this would be hard to ask, but I was going to push through the pressure just to let it go and ask her.

I prayed myself up and waited until a day Cindy seemed to feel good, as those days were few far and few in between. Then, like a kid, I saw an opening and began a conversation that I knew would lead to the question. She was attentive, and I believed she was on board until I asked her if we could go. Then, I heard the words I always dreaded, and she said, "Maybe so." Well, I knew what that meant in our language as a couple; that meant no. *Maybe so* was a response that we said instead of the word *no*, so we would not hurt each other's feelings. This is something that we have done for as long as we have known each other.

I was disappointed, but I was not going to give up after hearing that. I had a burning in my heart urging me not to give in and to continue to pray. I did just that and prayed for hours at a time for God to make a way. I knew going to church itself was not going to save anyone from anything, but the word I heard that night from God drove me to do what it took to get there. I did not know how or when, but I knew it would happen.

I let a couple of weeks pass by, and then I approached her again, but this time with more urgency in my voice, and I let her know that this was something I wanted to do and to please consider it. She smiled at me and said, "Sure, let's try it, and let's go Sunday." My heart exploded with joy. I thanked her and gave her a big hug. That night was the most restful sleep I'd had in such a long time, with the anticipation of what God had in store for us that Sunday. As the day approached, I was like a kid waiting on Christmas morning.

To many people, going to church would be no big deal, and they would look forward to the message ending so they could get to the restaurant before anyone else did. It was not so with me, as I felt this could very well be the beginning of a new life without the demonic spirits in my house. As the days ticked by the following week, my anxiety rose. My biggest concern was whether we would feel welcomed. I once visited a church for the first time, and a greeter handed me a pile of bulletins to hand out so they could go sit down. As you can imagine, I did not go back the following Sunday. I knew Cindy would be more nervous than I, and this could be our last opportunity for deliverance.

I went to bed on Saturday night with the jitters and did not know what was in store for us the next day. We had planned the 11:30 a.m. service so that Cindy would have the most time to sleep and get ready. I got up before sunrise to go outside with my coffee on the front porch. The morning light was just beautiful seeing it from my 184-year-old porch. There was an electric feeling in my soul for the first time in many years, and all seemed well. The plan was that Cindy would rise at 9:00 a.m. and prepare for church. We planned nothing fancy, and I figured if they disapproved of blue jeans and a Tee- shirt, then I had probably heard wrong from God.

Sunday morning arrived, and so did my anxiety. Would Cindy be able to wake up, and what other roadblocks were coming our way? I got up early and went outside to pray for what was to come. My heart leaped as I heard Cindy moving around upstairs. The thoughts of a better life consumed me so much that I busied myself taking care of anything that could delay or stop it from happening. Have you ever heard of anyone that checked the oil in a new car to be sure before they made a fifteen-minute ride down the road?

We headed out to church with my heart full of joy. I smiled as I knew the devil could not stop us now, and hopefully something good would happen to turn our ship around from the absolute hell we were experiencing here. We were going down the road when our new Jeep Cherokee engine suddenly cut off, and now we were sitting in the middle of the road. Was it a genuine mechanical issue or some supernatural attempt to stop us? After everything we had gone through all these years, I had an idea. We both looked at each other, not knowing what to do, so I said,

"Let's pray." We joined hands, both fervently praying in the Spirit, and I pressed the key button, and it cranked right up.

We arrived at the church relieved, but very stressed out. Remember, one of my concerns was whether we would feel welcome. We did not know anyone other than Tracy, who I called, and we had told no one we were coming. To our surprise, a neighbor of ours greeted us at the front door. She reached out to hug Cindy, and it was now clear that God had plans for us that day. We came in and found a seat to attend the service.

After the worship service, we sat down to hear the message, and so far, I was enjoying the service but had no idea what was on Cindy's mind. All the years of staying at home on Sundays and the troubles of the spirits that came to our house flooded my mind. Was there anything the pastor could say that would ease our hearts? We were attending one of the smaller satellite churches where the message was telecasted and shown on a large screen from the main campus. I knew from the internet the senior pastor was speaking to thousands of people and could not even know we were there, but the local campus pastor did come up to greet us before the service and made us feel welcome.

The message began with similar things like Scriptures and stories you hear from many churches, but there was something different about this one. I have sat in church services for years and could not recall how a message engrossed me. I soaked in every word but still wondered how God would use this experience to help us to rid the spirits from our plantation. Midway through the message, the pastor stopped preaching and said, "I don't usually do this, but God wants me to pray right now." He went on to say, "Someone has been struggling for years with anxiety and depression, and this day God is going to begin a new life for you." I know thousands had to receive that word from God, but today I knew God was speaking directly to Cindy and me. We raised our hands high to allow the prayer into our lives. We left church that morning with a renewed hope we had not felt in many years.

Chapter Sixteen:
The Deliverance Day Arrives

And He said to them, "I saw Satan fall like lightning from heaven. Behold, I give you the authority to trample on serpents and scorpions, and over all the power of the enemy, and nothing shall by any means hurt you. Nevertheless do not rejoice in this, that the spirits are subject to you, but rather rejoice because your names are written in heaven."

Luke 10:18–20

We had attended about three Sunday services and were enjoying everything about it. We met a few folks, and everyone was friendly to us so far. We arrived and met up with Tracy, who had saved us a couple seats so we could sit with her and her husband, Jimmy. I was standing up as the music started playing, and a man I had never met walked up and said, "This is going to be your day, and you will not have to spend another night in that house with them." He had a look in his eyes that gave me chills. I had no clue who he was nor what he was talking about. He quickly walked away after he spoke those words. My focus went back to the service, but the thought of what had just happened didn't leave my mind. The service ended, and Cindy and I headed to the car to go home. We returned to the car, and my thoughts returned to Zoe, our dog. It was all we could do to leave her at the house, knowing that the evil spirits were still there. I know it is not the typical thought process of most people who attend church, but it was ours.

We got back home, found everything was alright and went downstairs to eat our lunch. We talked a bit about the service and how encouraging it was. I was so glad that we maybe had found a place that would at least give us a couple of hours' breaks from the dark reality we faced daily in our home. After I had eaten my lunch, I looked at my phone to see that there were eight missed calls from Tracy. Wondering what was so important, I gave her a callback, and she asked if she and a few church members could come over to pray over our house. I didn't know what she meant by praying over our house, but I asked Cindy, and she agreed to let them come. We decided to meet at 3:00 p.m., and before we hung up, she asked us not to clean up or do anything to prepare for them. I was now getting a bit anxious about what was about to happen, but I was also glad that someone cared enough to take a Sunday afternoon to come and pray with us.

I was a little embarrassed by the mess in the kitchen, but we did what they asked and left the house just as it was. At 3:00 p.m., the church members began to arrive, and the only one I knew was Tracy. We went outside to meet everyone, and then a white truck pulled up with a man named Randy, who had spoken to me that morning in the service. They asked to gather outside in a circle, and I assumed that would be where they would pray for our house. I could tell that a lady named Kim and Randy seemed to be the leaders. Randy had a fire in his eyes and told us he was mad about what Tracy had told him at church. He said Tracy had approached him to pray for us before the service and told him about our full-time demonic house occupants. Randy said that God spoke to him not just to pray, but also to gather a group of prayer warriors to take them on in person with His anointing power. Kim explained that many more were praying for us, and only people without fear were to come over here.

Kim and Randy then explained what was about to happen. They said we would have communion, and then he and Kim would go inside the house. Everyone else was to stay outside and pray for us. Now they had gotten our attention fully, as we knew that it would not be a friendly Sunday afternoon prayer service but a demonic house cleansing.

We went from a few church members coming over to pray for us in just a few minutes to a full-fledged attack on the demonic spirits that had made our lives pure hell for over six years here at Springhill Plantation. What would they see, and what would they hear? I knew what they were going up against and that the spirits would not leave without a fight. My thoughts went back to all our encounters with them over the years and how we alone could not seem to get them out for good. We were born-again Christians, so why were we chosen to be under such a fierce attack? What was the open door that allowed them to return after we commanded them to leave using the name of Jesus? Why did they ignore the anointing oil all over the house? I also thought of what this meeting would cause if it did not work. Cindy and I, even though going to the church a few times, were still on the edge of hopelessness. Mentally tired was not a good description of our situation, as we were exhausted from the coming and going of the spirits that inhabited our home.

We gathered in the circle to start the house cleansing, with everyone laying hands on us and praying for the power of God to fall on the house and us. Kim then brought out the communion cups with the wafers and juice and handed them to all of us. Next, Tracy began to speak over us a Scripture that the Lord had put into her heart:

And if one prevail against him, two shall withstand him, and a threefold cord is not quickly broken.

Ecclesiastes 4:12 KJV

That scripture began to burn into my soul, and my mind began to think it could be one of the missing pieces of the puzzle. The fear began to leave me, and a spark of faith started to rise in me. Jesus spoke that having faith the size of a mustard seed was enough to move a mountain. So indeed, this mountain we had prayed for so long to leave could be crumbling before our very eyes. I was laser-focused on what was happening around me, and I knew this would be a day I would never forget for the rest of my life.

Before we started the communion service, another lady named Paulette wanted to speak a few words. She asked us to stand facing each other, and with a firm tone in her voice, she looked at me and said, "I know you have unforgiveness in your heart toward someone," and none of what we were doing today was going to work until I dealt with it. She asked who it was. How did she know that, as nobody there knew our story since six of the seven, I only met for the first time that afternoon? My chest was pounding as I pointed toward Cindy and told Paulette it was her that I had unforgiveness towards. She then asked Cindy the same question and got the same response that Cindy had unforgiveness towards me. A hush overcame everyone as God revealed a dirty little secret nobody could have known. All the years of struggle had caused a deep bitterness to form between us. We were never on the same page about what we wanted in the relationship. I wanted to be closer, and she wanted the same thing, but I did not realize I was not the kind of husband anyone would wish to have a more intimate relationship with.

Paulette then said before we go any further, we must deal with this. So, I looked into Cindy's eyes and asked her to forgive me for what I had done to her. She said that she would, and she asked the same of me. We then embraced each other for a long time. The chains of unforgiveness were falling off, and now it was time to have communion with a clean heart. I can't tell you how often I took the Lord's communion with unforgiveness and open sin in my life and couldn't figure out why nothing changed, and instead things even got worse.

Communion began as Kim handed out the cups with wafers, and she was amazed as there were precisely seven of them in her bag. She said in a rush to get things ready she just grabbed a handful of them and did not know how many people were coming. We knew that was a sign from heaven that a holy war would happen in our house and our lives that day. There were too many things falling into place for this to be a manufactured event, and you could physically feel the electricity of God's presence all over the place. We then took the body and the blood of Jesus, and then it was time for war.

Randy took the lead and told us he and Kim were going into the house to drive them out. Nobody was to come in, no matter what we heard or saw. He was leaving the back door open to make way for the spirits to exit, and we were to stay away from it. Kim would follow him, speaking Scriptures over the house and us. Randy did not walk but ran toward the house, shouting God's praises as they both entered the back door. You could hear the battle going on loudly from inside, with the tangible presence of angels felt all around, and the three left outside were fervently praying over us. I could not imagine what the demonic spirits were feeling, knowing that the house they had called home for maybe as long as 184 years was under attack, and they were the targets. You could hear Randy and Kim shouting Jesus' name, not in English but in Hebrew translation YESHUA.

We did not see or hear it, but we felt an evil presence exit the house from the back door. Randy and Kim left the main home and headed to the Little House. There always has been a connection to that place that was evil. That was where my friend Chris heard the voice in the dark asking when he was awake yet and where the carpenter whose tools came up missing. During a power outage at her house, my daughter came over to stay in it. It lasted one hour before she told us she would rather sit in the dark than stay there. We continued to pray as Randy and Kim entered and left the door open. The intensity increased with each passing minute as the battle raged between God and the demonic spirits. It felt more like they were fleeing from one place to another than fighting back. The main house was clean, but now they were in the hospital.

Kim and Randy were only in the hospital for a few minutes, but I could feel the negative energy come out. The shouting coming from Randy and Kim had become so loud that I thought the neighbors would hear it, though I couldn't have cared less as I watched the most incredible experience, I had ever had in my life unfolding in front of me. The Scripture in Ecclesiastes of the threefold cord was coming to pass as we all stood outside. Cindy and I had been fighting this battle alone for a long time. But now, there was an army of Christians at my house and other places, praying at that very moment for our deliverance.

The last place left was the barn, and now Randy and Kim were on the way over there to get after it. If you remember, earlier in this book, the barn was where I saw the fog come out and cross over the driveway to enter the hospital when we first moved in. It was also where I saw the spirit I called "The 1800s Gentleman" stand over Cindy while she was feeding the cats. I can't tell you what connection the barn had with the spirits, but there must have been something that happened in the past to cause them to want to stay there. There was an experience Kim had in there that I will let her tell you in her own words at the end of the chapter, but it was almost unbelievable. The power of God was now exploding with supernatural energy that was hard to comprehend. Nothing could stop the anointing of God that day, and the spirits fled from one place to another with nowhere left to go.

Randy and Kim finished by walking around our property's outer parts, praising and shouting the name of YESHUA. I had cattle on my place, and as they walked past them, my two-thousand-pound bull began to snort and leaped up into the air, threatening to charge them. Maybe that was an attempt by the spirits to place fear into their hearts, but it was not to be as Kim kept on praying and never wavered. We all gathered back into the circle and began praising God for the victory.

I did not have a clue that this would be the day I had prayed for years for it to happen. Even though I had gotten fragile in spirit and hope was about to fade away, I always knew my God was with me. After everyone left, Cindy and I went back inside and felt a sense of peace like we had never experienced. This time it was different, as we knew, unlike before, we had the backing of a group of people with the love of God for their fellow brothers and sisters in Christ. A sense of power lingered around our place, and we basked in it. Never before had we known without a doubt there was a God who loves us and cares deeply for us. We may go through confusing and demanding times, but if we trust Him, He will walk us through anything. I realized for the first time that we cannot always pray to make our problems instantly go away, but there is a place in Him where we can go and have peace despite our troubles.

The church invited us to a cookout at the pastor's farm that evening. We excitedly accepted and later drove over to see hundreds of fellow Christians gathering for a meal and fellowship. Only a few knew what happened that day, but we were surrounded by many with the love of Christ as we had never experienced. They could see that we have been suffering through hell for years. I could see this was a church filled with praying and caring believers with a purpose in life to help others. I had a grin on my face that nothing could wipe it off. The cookout was on a cattle farm in the barn, and even though I stepped in cow manure with my new shoes, it was the best time ever. We now belonged somewhere, and our life of being alone was over.

Let's hear directly from them, their experiences.

TRACY

God has gifted me with the gift of hospitality. I am, by nature, a connector of people. My role in this story was as an intercessor for Eric and Cindy. When Eric reached out to me and told me how he and Cindy were being spiritually attacked, I knew that I was not equipped to provide them guidance, but I knew how to connect them to the right people. I asked Eric if it was okay to reach out to my friend at church. He assured me that it was fine and asked that we pray for them. He told me how they had not been in fellowship or attending church in several years. I invited them to join us the following Sunday.

As God ordained, my husband and I were co-leading a small group. A week prior, our small group had a conversation about spiritual attacks. We had discussed Ephesians 6:12, "For our struggles are not against flesh and blood, but against the rulers, against the powers of this dark world and against the spiritual forces of evil in the heavenly realms."

I immediately reached out to my friend and spiritual mentor, Kim. I shared with her the details of how satan was attacking Eric and Cindy. They were living in spiritual isolation and were being attacked on all fronts. They were in desperate need of spiritual intervention. I know that God's word is true and faithful.

The Lord directs the steps of the godly. He delights in every detail of our lives. Though we stumble, we will not fall, for the Lord holds us by the hand.

Psalm 37:23–24 NLT

In their hearts, humans plan their course, but the Lord establishes their steps.

Proverbs 16:9 NIV

I know that God had directed Eric to me in this specific time, with a very specific need. My role was to intercede in prayer for them and to help connect them to the people that God prepared for this very moment.

God placed a second person on my heart to reach out to and share Eric and Cindy's situation. On Sunday morning, prior to our worship service, I shared with Randy how Eric and Cindy were being attacked spiritually and how they were living in isolation and trying to fight on their own. They had become spiritually tired and were living under constant attacks by satan which had led to anxiety, depression and physical ailments.

Randy was so moved by the impact the attacks had caused on Eric and Cindy's lives. He immediately knew that God was calling him to get involved and to intervene on their behalf. We could see that satan had them right where he wanted them. They were isolated from friends, church and spiritual support. It is in isolation that satan does his greatest work.

Ecclesiastes 4:9–10 NIV says, "Two are better than one, because they have a good return for their labor. If either of them falls down, one can help the other up. But pity anyone and has no one to help them. Also, if two lie down together, they will keep warm. But how can one keep warm alone? Though one may be overpowered, two can defend themselves. A cord of three strands is not quickly broken."

God was putting together a network of people to intervene and be the hands and feet of Jesus. I saw people who were willing to empty out themselves and carry out God's ministry to two people that they had only just met. I saw others who used their gift of prayer to intercede in the situation. Still others used their abilities to encourage and call out leadership qualities and skills. I was able to use my gift of being a connector and leading Eric and Cindy to spiritual leaders that they were desperately in need of.

I have watched in awe as God has worked in and through Eric and Cindy and delivered them out of spiritual darkness and isolation to freedom. I see two beautiful people that are now joyful and hopeful. They are now surrounded by a family of believers and are now connected to a network of support and love. I believe that God is going to use and commission them to open doors for others to be freed from spiritual isolation and attacks.

To God be the glory!

KIM

I will tell you, Eric, that I have never felt such opposition in my whole life like in your house. Those spirits did not want us there. And I've never prayed in tongues with such authority or power. It was not scary, but it was really heavy. I felt the presence of the Holy Spirit come down on me and Randy, which made us feel as strong as a heavyweight champion lifter. I left your farm with a complete understanding of the blood atonement poured out for us.

The things that stood out the most were when the bull snorted at me and followed me down the fence line and when the tools in the shed moved like a breeze had passed through them, but there was no wind. Randy never wavered in his commands, and I never ceased reading the Word over your farm. It was beautiful carrying out God's Word with such fierce power. When that happens, it's like an out-of-body experience. I heard the reading of His Word, and it spoke over me with awe; not like I could do anything, but it was manifested through me. It's all about obedience and submission to God's Word and the testament of Jesus' mission to teach us by example. You, too, will be used to free others from such oppression. And so will Cindy.

PAULETTE

What I remember the most about that day I came to help pray for your home and your family was the brokenness in you and your wife and how desperate you all were for a change. I felt like maybe you all had reached the end of your rope, and you knew that God was the only way, perhaps even having doubts about what would take place. That's the reason we prayed over things in your life that needed to be broken and for God to bring deliverance to you both, but there's one thing that I prayed more than anything: that God would show you that He had done it and that all of you would know that it was only God and not man. We were there as His vessels, but He has done all the work and deserves all the glory and honor for what took place in your lives, home, and family. I praise God for that; I know you will have a great testimony. I'm so proud that you are writing this book that will touch many lives and help them because many people out there feel hopeless simply because of the evilness in this world, but with God, all things are possible. There's nothing impossible with God.

RANDY

I woke up on Sunday morning expecting to go to church to worship God and learn from His Word, but I did not know that God had much more in store for me that day. So, I headed to church as usual, and when I arrived, I checked in with our dream team on that day as I was due to work safety during the second service. While I was outside, I was approached by another member of the church named Tracy. She motioned me to come over to her; so, I did and asked what she needed. I could see in her eyes she was deeply troubled about something. Tracy told me of someone who needed prayer about a situation at their home. I said sure I would pray and asked what the problem was. Tracy then told me she was contacted by a man named Eric, who lived in the area and just had started coming to church.

She told me they were experiencing demonic attacks in the plantation home they owned, which was wrecking their lives. I told her I sure would pray for them this morning while in church. I walked away to continue my safety job that morning for church and began to pray for them. I had not met them and did not know who they were, but a wave of holy anger overcame me when I prayed. I heard a word from God that startled me as He told me that just praying would not be enough this time. I could not get past it and asked God what He was saying to me. God told me this day; you and others are to go and drive the demons out of that house. God said they were not to spend another night with the demons and to gather those who He had chosen strong in spirit to go that very afternoon.

I started weeping uncontrollably, and chills went all over my body. That word from God consumed me, and I couldn't even go into the service that was about to begin. I asked God who I was supposed to ask to go as I knew this was a big deal and lives were on the line this day. Then a name came up in my spirit, and it was Kim. I sent Tracy to get her, and we filled her in on what was happening. I asked her if she would be willing to go with us, and she said she was waiting for the opportunity to rise and minister in this realm. She said, "Let's go!"

I asked Tracy what Eric and Cindy looked like, and Tracy told me they would be sitting with her. I don't remember going into the service, but I was told I went up to them and said, "This is going to be your day," and then I went back outside to pray more. I called my wife, who was on a trip to visit family, and told her what I was about to do. She was stunned and asked if I was sure I wanted to do this, and I said this was something I had to do. I asked her to begin praying at 3:00 p.m. when everyone would meet at the house. While outside, something inside me was trying to talk me out of going through this. I felt unworthy and asked God why He would choose me for something like this. Before I was born again, I was a drug addict and I also manufactured drugs and sold them.

I felt the need to talk to my mentor, who knew all about the ministry of deliverance. His name was Jay, and he also attended our church. I met him outside and asked if I could call him after he got home. He said yes and that he already knew what was going on. I thought that was strange as nobody had told him anything as he was at the service while all this was happening. I waited for a little before I gave him a call. Jay answered, and I told him the story. He said he felt a prick in his spirit that God would move that day concerning church members. I asked him to go, but he said no because his ministry was to stay back to pray in the spirit.

He told me I was to go into the house and advised me on

handling this cleansing.

Jay gave me three things to accomplish.

(1) Read Genesis 3:15 and speak it repeatedly.

And I will put enmity between you and the woman, and between your offspring and hers; he will crush your head, and you will strike his heel.

Genesis 3:15 NIV

(2) Take the authority that God gave you and go inside with no fear.

(3) Leave the back door open as you enter the house.

I headed to the Davis's plantation home, and a battle was going through my mind. One was the knowledge of the power of God inside of me, and the other was the fear that something terrible might happen to me inside that house. I recalled in Acts 19:15–16 where demons attacked some Jews, attempting to cast them out using the name of Jesus although they were not Christians. The demons overpowered them, and they ran out beaten and naked. I then got a hold of myself, knowing this was nothing but satan making a strong attempt to stop what God was about to do. Boldness welled up inside of me as I arrived at the house.

I got out of my truck to meet with the other church members who had already arrived. I saw Eric and Cindy standing with the others and the hopelessness in their eyes. They also looked exhausted and so beat down, and even though I had not met them, I felt a kindred spirit between them and me. I went to them and asked if they had been born again, and they both said yes. Cindy had been a Christian her whole life, and Eric said he had been for thirty-five years. A rage boiled in my soul at how satan could do this to such good Christians. The doubt was gone, and it was time to eject these evil spirits away from them and their lovely plantation home.

After the prayer and communion, Kim, with her Bible in hand, and I headed to the back door, looking back at Eric and Cindy before entering. We felt an overwhelming heaviness and a powerful resistance when we entered the house. Kim was loudly speaking the Word of God, and I was shouting for them to get out in the name of Yeshua. While Kim was speaking the Word, she was also praying in tongues. We had not been in the house but a few seconds when God's incredible power fell on us. While we were there, we could not see them, but we knew they were hiding inside the house. Yes, I said, hiding as they were now giving no resistance but more like trying to get away from the power of God.

We headed upstairs first, planning to clear the top floor and work ourselves down. We anointed every door and the pictures of the family we found as we battled the demons upstairs. We approached a closet on the top floor and sensed something evil was behind that door. With authority, I opened that door and commanded the demons to get out in the name of Yeshua. We both knew the top floor was free of demons and took the battle downstairs, and when we entered the living room, I could feel one standing in front of a hurricane lamp in a bay window. I could feel the electricity in my hands as I pointed them to leave, and when I did, I felt it go right by me and out the door.

Kim and I left the main house and went over to the hospital. We entered and were met upstairs with powerful resistance. We spoke the name of Jesus, and in an instant, the presence of God filled the house. We praised God as we exited, and we knew they were gone.

The last building to pray over was the barn where Eric kept his tools. Kim and I went in with the oil and the Word of God spoken with authority. When we stepped into the entrance, the tools hanging on the pegs began to sway back and forth. But, unafraid, we pressed on with the name of Jesus and His Word. We shouted the praises of God, and victory came with explosive power as the demonic spirits departed the plantation.

Chapter Seventeen:
The Fight Wasn't Over

¹¹ And they overcame him by the blood of the Lamb and by the word of their testimony, and they did not love their lives to the death. ¹² Therefore rejoice, O heavens, and you who dwell in them! Woe to the inhabitants of the earth and the sea! For the devil has come down to you, having great wrath, because he knows that he has a short time."

Revelation 12:11-12

The next ten months after the house cleaning, we filled ourselves with the Word, worship, and fellowship with other believers. Every week we could feel ourselves getting a little stronger in faith and hope for a better future. However, there were still voices that spoke into our minds not to continue to go on this path. They would speak softly, saying, *"You are just setting yourselves up for failure by going back to church again."* Other times they would say, *"You have had a long week and you're tired, so it's okay not to go to church and to stay in bed."* We had to fight off the voices because some of what they said was true. We had issues with past church experiences and were tired from a long week at work.

We began to attend a small group from church that met on Thursday nights and who asked us to tell our stories. I was hesitant, to say the least, because of the past responses I received when the occurrences started years ago. I remembered the look on people's faces of terror, and some of them you knew they thought you must be crazy. Nevertheless, we reluctantly agreed because of the love and support we had received from many of them. I knew God wanted us to tell our story, but it was still a hard thing to do.

We arrived with a whole house of people ready to hear our testimony of how God delivered us from years of demonic attacks on our marriage, health, and minds. I am not a public speaker nor a preacher by no means, but still, I knew this was something we needed to do. I just told them what happened, and I held nothing back. I was a little shocked that nobody ran for their lives. Even more impressive was how others could relate to our account; even one lady had a similar experience. I was now seeing how we were not alone in how satan works, and he was attacking everyone differently. Even in that, I could see something in all these people that I had desperately wanted. They had peace about them even in the middle of the storms of life. Some had health and financial issues, and any other problem you can name; they still looked happy and at peace.

⁴⁴Then he says, 'I will return to my house from which I came.' And when he comes, he finds it empty, swept, and put in order. ⁴⁵*Then he goes and takes with him seven other spirits more wicked than himself, and they enter and dwell there; and the last state of that man is worse than the first. So shall it also be with this wicked generation."*

Matthew 12:44-45

It was almost a year since we had been attending church, filling ourselves with His anointing and Word. Our house has been so peaceful, and our lives are returning to what we would call normal. It was so relaxed now I was starting to wonder if there would ever be another attack on our lives. Would this be the way it was from now on? I knew better than that, as the Bible plainly says in John 16:33 that you will have tribulations, and I was unaware that very thing was coming soon.

It was a Saturday night; I was watching TV downstairs after doing outside chores all day. I could hear Cindy and Zoe, the rat terrier dog upstairs, moving around. I didn't know what they were doing, but I enjoyed the relaxation after a hot workday. Then, I heard Cindy coming down the stairs, and she had a look on her face that I had seen many times before but not for almost a year. With a tremble in her voice, Cindy sat down on the couch and told me the spirits were back. I asked what happened as I had felt nothing in the house and was surprised by this news. However, I did not doubt her words and knew she was keen on these spirits after all these years. She told me she had a feeling for a few days, was upstairs, and heard Zoe making noises in the bedroom. She went in to see what she was doing and witnessed something holding her down on the bed. She could not see the thing but could see Zoe was terrified and fighting back to get free. Cindy ran to the bed and grabbed Zoe while rebuking that thing in Jesus's name!

The standard protocol for something like this was to get the anointing oil and get after it with prayer and using the name of Jesus. This time I had the urge to step back for a moment and get some wise counsel before making any moves. If you remember, a man named Randy led the house cleaning a year ago. I called him to inform him of the situation and see if he would come over to assist. He told me he was out of town and could not come, but wanted to call someone he knew that was his mentor in that type of ministry. I was unaware that during the initial house cleaning a year ago that this was the man that gave instructions to Randy. He advised how to handle coming into our home and dealing with these demons.

I was enraged that the demons would attack our little dog Zoe. In all the past attacks, they would go after whoever was the weakest, whether mental or physical. Most of the time, it was Cindy, as she was the one who struggled the most with anxiety and depression. Sometimes it was me as I would sometimes listen to lies the voices in my head would say. But to try to hurt our Zoe, who was completely innocent, was more than I could take. We prayed over the house and waited for Randy to give us a callback. Later that evening, Randy did call to tell me that his mentor Jay wanted us to come over to his house after church the next day and that he had a word from the Lord concerning our trouble.

After we prayed over the house, it seemed clear, but we knew that we would have to face them again soon, with a new revelation that we would hear from Jay the next day. We went to church, and afterward, I met Randy to head over to Jay's house. We arrived, and after some small talk, we went inside to discuss what Jay had from the Lord. Talking to Jay, I could easily see He was a man of God and had been through many encounters with demons through the years. I felt a kindred type spirit with him and deep respect. Knowing I was talking to someone who had been through what we had gone through but came out on the other side victorious was a great feeling of joy. He was a hard man and did not mince words about what we were facing, but that was the exact thing I wanted to hear.

Jay asked me to start from the beginning, so I told him everything that we had experienced and went into detail. Jay said he had been praying in the Spirit since he heard from Randy the day before and did have a word from God for us. He told us that from a year ago, he knew at some point that they would try to get back into our house and, this time, would try to destroy us for good. He said that some spirits had lived in this house since the 1800s. He told me their leader had been following us since we were married in 1988. When he said that, it caused a memory to come back to my mind of an experience I had a few months after we got married.

Soon after we were married, we moved into a small mobile home. It was our first home, and as newlyweds, our life was just beginning. We attended a tiny Methodist Church not far from our house, the same church my parents and grandparents attended. A few months after we moved in, I began to have nightmares. The dreams of a tall black ghostly figure would stand in front of my bed and just stare at me even though it had no eyes. I would awaken having night sweats and a terrible panic attack. I was having the same type of trouble that the kids in the movie *"A Nightmare on Elm Street"* were having, as going to sleep was something I feared doing. I was not seeing Freddie Kruger with his bladed gloves but the tall, dark demonic figure nightly. A few weeks into having these nightmares were getting to me and wondering how to say something to Cindy about this. My thoughts were, *"Would she have regrets about getting married to me?"*

One night I woke up from a bad dream fully alert only to see in absolute horror that a black figure was standing right in front of me. I was not having a nightmare anymore but a real-life event happening right before me. The rest of the night, I went sleepless and full of fear. The next night I went to bed hoping that the night before did not happen, even though I knew it did. Just like the night before, I awoke to the ghostly black figure staring at me at the foot of our bed. I tried to scream but could not make a sound and could not understand how Cindy could sleep while something like this was happening in our bedroom.

That was all I could take, and I asked Cindy if I could confide in her about what was happening. I was nervous but did manage to tell her what was going on. I told her about the nightly visitations from the black figure I was having, and to my surprise, she did not say I was crazy but asked me one question. *Had I ever given my life to Jesus and asked to be born again?* Never have I appreciated Cindy more than that day with such wisdom from God. I have been attending church for 24 years and thought that being a good person and believing that there was a God was good enough to get to heaven. I read later in James 2:19 that even the demons believe the same thing and shudder. We called the pastor of our small church and told him about our experience, and I think he was a bit shocked but came right over to lead me into the prayer of repentance, and I gave my heart to Jesus that very day. The dark figure was the same one attacking us in our house here on the plantation, and I recognized him as the boss spirit I saw in our bedroom a year ago.

Jay began to speak to me about what was happening and why. He told me that the demons indeed fled when the church came over that day to cleanse our house, but they still believed they had ownership of the house. They were watching us from afar as we continued to go to church, and we ignored their voices to stop the path we were on. However, they saw we were getting more robust in the word, and our faith grew weekly. We now had more believers coming beside us who knew about our testimony, and the spirits were going to make a last-ditch move on us to see if we had enough faith and power of the Holy Ghost to take them on ourselves. If we gave in to fear, they would have us and our house back as they had for over a century.

Jay told me that Cindy and I were to take the lead, and Randy would be just there for support, unlike last time the church came in, and we stayed outside being prayed over by the rest. I knew Cindy and I did have the power of God and the backing of our church on our sides. He then told me something compelling that he got from God. He said we were to call them out by name, and I asked him to clarify his meaning. He told us that the four leading spirits operating at our house were the spirit of anxiety, the spirit of depression, the spirit of fear, and lastly, a liar spirit. We were to leave the back door open as we entered the house, go to the second floor, and have communion together before doing anything. He gave me some anointing oil he had used for many of his demonic battles, and I was to apply it to the doors and windows as we moved throughout the house.

We went upstairs to begin the battle for our house and ourselves. We started with communion and then used the anointing oil on all of us, including Zoe, our dog. Afterward, we began to all pray in the Spirit, and a powerful anointing like I had never felt before fell on all three of us. Cindy had the word of God speaking words of life over the house, and Randy was shouting for them to leave in the name of Yeshua, the original Hebrew name of Jesus. I was calling them out by their spirit's name. I screamed out to the spirit of anxiety to bow down to the name of Yeshua and immediately flee the house. I called out to the spirit of depression to bow down to Yeshua's name and get out of the house. I called them out by name and commanded them to leave and never to return to this house again.

As we prayed, there was no fight or resistance at all this time. The spirits hit the first-floor door in less time than I spoke out their spirit names, and we all could sense the total peace that enveloped the house. The confidence of knowing who we are in Christ is a powerful thing to possess. I have never known what the scripture 1 John 4:4 meant until now, *"You are of God, little children, and have overcome them, because He who is in you is greater than he who is in the world."* I do have the greater one living in me!

It's been almost two years now since the evil spirits were driven out of this house. Cindy and I worked together so that there were no more open doors that could allow them back. We, as a couple, are now more bonded together than we ever have been since we were married. We still have issues like any married couple or anyone experiences, but now there is a revelation of God's power and plan for our lives. We are vigilant and keep our guard against any subtle attack from them.

Chapter Eighteen
Let's Put This All Together

Come now, and let us reason together, saith the Lord: though your sins be as scarlet, they shall be as white as snow; though they be red like crimson, they shall be as wool.
Isaiah 1:18 (KJV)

Have you ever amid a life's storm questioned where God was and why? Well, I would say you would be in good company as my family, and I did for years and sometimes still do to this day! The above scripture I found says Its just fine to ask God why and where he is when something terrible is happening in your life. As a father and a husband, I can relate when I see my family in pain, and they don't understand why trouble is happening. In a world where every day you can easily see satans influence it can be sometimes hard to know that Gods explosive power is still very much in control and His presence is everywhere. Just the fact that you just took a breath of air into your lungs should be enough to convince you. I everyday must put my trust in God, and I can say after all these years it's still sometimes hard not to attempt to fix everything myself instead of giving it to God.

After this experience that took us to the edge, we knew we must always be aware of the enemy's tricks and schemes and never allow another foothold back into our lives and home. We both have taken the time to pray and ask God what he wanted us to know about this battle and why it was allowed to happen. You notice I said, "It was allowed to happen." I had reflected on when Cindy and I first met and have received revelations that there were signs of trouble all along.

If you recall, back at the beginning of this book, I brought into my home a statue given to me in Massachusetts. I felt something wrong the whole time I had it with me on the trip home, but my selfish desire to keep it, knowing that Cindy objected, opened a door of trouble into our home. I now know that that statue must have had some type of demonic curse. The first signs of activity began when it was brought into our house. Another thing was I was not the spiritual leader of our family; Cindy was. My thoughts were trained on work and doing fun things alone, like fishing and hunting. There is nothing wrong with none of those things, but I neglected my family's emotional and spiritual needs as I focused on those things. I even went on a weekend hunting trip the week after I got married, leaving my beautiful new bride at home by herself. How selfish is that? I also allowed myself to be dictated to by other family members, and from fear of rejection, I did not take a stand for what was suitable for Cindy and our daughter.

At every stage of my life, I have bowed to others to

ensure I did not hurt any feelings knowing what was right but submitting instead. God is faithful and has always put warnings into my path. Do you recall the dream of the lions earlier in this book? I had that dream in 2010, which was a direct warning of things to come if I did not step up and change my life direction, which I did not. I let others dictate my path and decisions, not God, and when I allowed that, it put my family and me on the rocky road that led us here.

Chapter Nineteen
Second Chances & Supporting Hands

The Lord is not slack concerning His promise, as some count slackness, but is longsuffering toward us, not willing that any should perish but that all should come to repentance.

2 Peter 3:9

As I reflect on everything that happened here over the years, there is one thing that was always the same. God never left or stopped attempting to guide us through the valley we found ourselves in. Even though I believe I caused most of the issues, God was always there with His faithfulness and grace showing us the way out. He allowed us to get to the edge of the ledge, and when I cried out in agony for His mercy that night after seeing the demonic spirit in the office window was the point of contact that God required for our deliverance. That was the first time I truly gave God my troubles and stopped trying to fix everything myself. We had tried to do this alone with no help from anyone. Instead, He used the local Church believers to come to alongside us. They used their gifts of the spirit to go into battle on our behalf.

I want to make sure you know that it was the blood of Jesus that delivered us from the demonic Spirits not the church. Churches do not have the power to save anyone as only Gods power can do that. If going to church was all we needed, then none of this would have ever happened. Becoming a part of the body of Christ and attending Church is important. It's something every believer needs to do to grow in faith and come together to worship God as a family. We found out the hard way that if you believe you can fight the forces of evil alone you are going to have a difficult road ahead of you.

In the Bible, you see multiple accounts of God using simple everyday people who have made terrible decisions in their life. The apostle Paul sought out and killed Christians, and God used him mightily for the Gospel. King David, who God used to slay Goliath, the giant, ended up committing adultery with Bathsheba. If that was not bad enough, he had her husband sent to the front lines to be killed so he could have Bathsheba as his wife. God delivered him and then called him his friend. God will deliver you no matter what you have done badly in life.

In Luke 23:39-43 is the account of Jesus hanging on the cross between two criminals. One of them was hurling insults at Jesus but the other asked Jesus to remember him when he entered the kingdom of heaven. Jesus told him that day he would be with him in Paradise. That thief never got baptized, never attended a day in church and did not give a penny in the offering plate but made it to heaven. If Jesus accepted him just as he was then he will not only accept you he will also deliver from what the enemy is currently attacking you with.

My prayer and purpose for writing this book are to encourage others who may be in the same situation as we were and to let them know that God is with them and will never leave them in the middle of a storm. If you feel you are currently under some spiritual attack, then consider that just maybe you could be a threat to the devil and God has a purpose for your life that you don't even know about yet. If you still have a heartbeat, then you have a purpose. I truly believe God opened my eyes to see and hear the things we did to be a testimony of the enemy's schemes and declared the blood of Jesus as the answer. All Cindy and I wanted in this life was to live peacefully and comfortably, but God had other plans and I am grateful He did. If our testimony helps one person get the deliverance they so desperately want, then our purpose in life has been worth it.

Though one may be overpowered by another, two can withstand him. And a threefold cord is not quickly broken.
Ecclesiastes 4:12

You cannot do this alone, and God did not create you to fight battles all by yourself. The enemy slowly, step by step, eased us into believing we needed nobody. We left our church and decided it was time to take a break from the weekly grind of attending services. Vacations are fine and needed to reset your mind, but a permanent vacation from other believers is all the enemy needs to wreck your life. The dream I had of the lions separating my wife, daughter, and I was a sign from God that satan had plans to disconnect us from the family of believers. Satan was almost successful, and we paid a high price for it.

In 2014 when our marriage was in shambles, we attended a marriage counseling intensive in Georgia. When we arrived, it was time for the evening meal. There were five couples there, and as we sat around the table, the other couples were laughing and holding hands, and it seemed like they did not have a care in the world. I was somewhat confused about what I was seeing because Cindy and I were attending to help save our marriage. Were we the only ones that had struggles? During that week, I realized that everyone there had something terrible going on in their marriages and personal lives, but they were very good at hiding it. We now knew that the couple walking hand in hand down the street could be in trouble with their marriage and near divorce. The person with that big house and all the money in the world suffers from depression. Another couple who, in your opinion, may have nothing and are poor were at peace and living better than we were. We all have a story of the highs and lows in our lives, no matter who we are. We live in a highly complicated world these days, and during that week, we all figured out that telling our stories helped us all understand that we are not alone and need each other in life.

While sitting in Georgia, my thoughts went back to what was going on at our home. A big sign on the wall at the Marriage center said, "IT'S ALL CONNECTED." I believe

God was even at that time trying to get my attention to say that we are not created to be alone to face the issues that will surely come our way. We need each other as we may be weak in one area, then we can lean on another who is strong. We were commanded to encourage each other in the faith, but how can you receive encouragement or give it by sitting at home all by yourselves?

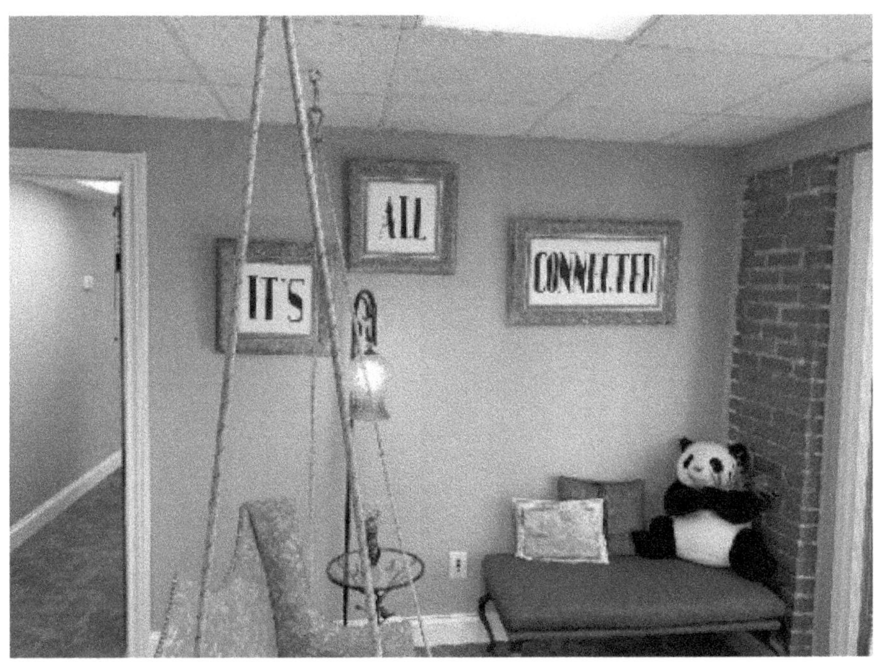

The church whom I heard in my spirit that night is who God sent our way to walk beside us while we were weak in faith and under fierce attack from satan. The believers make up the church, and our problem was that we were a one-member church that believed we needed no others to receive what God had for us.

After high school, I joined the military and did training with thousands of other fellow soldiers. I will never forget arriving at basic training to be met by some of the most demanding drill instructors, I believe, who walked the planet. They were battle-tested in Vietnam and made it home after enduring the absolute hell of war. They had been hit by gunfire and wounded by grenades but never gave up, even when it looked impossible to make it out alive. The biggest lesson that we were taught was not what you would think. It was not how accurate you could shoot your rifle or even how great you were in hand-to-hand combat but how good of a teammate you could be. Strength in numbers and unity was the focus of most of my training. We celebrated victories together and would bind together during times of struggle. I knew if we ever had to fight in a war anywhere in this world, I would never have to look behind me because there was someone there ready to fight to make sure I made it out alive.

While I was in basic training, we would get up every morning and go for a run. Every day the runs would get longer and longer to build up your stamina. One morning we headed out while it was still pitch dark, expecting the same thing, but what I saw surprised me. I looked up and saw a tall mountain coming up in the distance. The sunrise began to shine, and I could see the drill instructors standing at the bottom with more at the top. I knew that I had a challenge ahead of me that would determine if I was a man or not. If you think the drill instructors were taking a break at the top and bottom, you would be wrong, as they were more than ran alongside us, urging us along with their fierce voices. The incline was almost straight up, and my heart felt like it was going to explode. I told myself to get to the top, and everything would be okay, not realizing my trip down would hurt worse.

As we arrived at the top, the drill instructors screamed to get back to the bottom of the mountain. I began the dissent to realize it was not much easier to go down due to the stress on your legs at that angle. You were not allowed to go at your own pace with the drill instructors right there in your face yelling. Halfway down, I turned my ankle and began rolling down the side of the mountain, and suddenly, I felt someone on top of me stopping my fall. I was picked up by two of my comrades whom I have never met, and they carried me to the bottom. They did for me what we, as Christians, are asked to do in Galatians 6:1. We are to bear each other's burdens. This experience I vividly remember to this day is a daily reminder to me of how we cannot have victory in our lives without the help of others.

Is that not how the church of God is supposed to be? I have been to churches I know would stand next to me in the middle of a storm, and I also have been to some I know they would not. Are you currently going to church? If so, can you say they would go to battle for you if you told them, you were experiencing the same thing we did? Does your church offer more than a few songs and a friendly message? The modern-day church I currently see does not say much about how demons are real and desire to destroy us and are on a last-day mission to do just that. I hear more about evil spirits on TV reality shows than I have in many Christian churches. If your church will fight for you, and you know you have fellow believers ready to come along your side if you have a mental health issue or physical health problem, then you are in a great place, but if you can't say that, then you will need to pray that God leads you to another church that does. There are churches in your area filled with loving believers ready to stand with you in this battle you are fighting. Do not let guilt or condemnation stop you from seeking another body of believers where you can receive the word of God and find your deliverance. We learned the hard way that you cannot do this alone because satan will take you down a lonely road that will cause misery and destruction.

Chapter Twenty
We Believed a Lie

You are of your father the devil, and the desires of your father you want to do. He was a murderer from the beginning, and does not stand in the truth, because there is no truth in him. When he speaks a lie, he speaks from his own resources, for he is a liar and the father of it.

John 8:44

Believing satan's lies was a primary cause of demons having their way here at our plantation. The lies we believed stole our focus on Jesus, and we spent most of our time here focused on the demons inside this house instead of God living in us. For years they consumed our thoughts, and we allowed them to control our emotions. As we let them do that, our physical body joined in with all kinds of issues, from headaches to panic attacks and numerous other health issues. I understand we may have had a situation many may not have, but that did not change the fact that God's word is life in every case.

When I was a young boy, I loved to fish at my grandfather's pond across the road from my house. I went almost every day during the summer break from school, and it was a hot day when I went over to fish. My grandfather also had cattle in that pasture where the pond was. I arrived, and as soon as my lure hit the water, I caught them one after another. Times were different back then, and even though there were cows in that pasture, I was allowed to go any time I wanted. I was having a great day catching fish and heard my mother calling me to come home for lunch. I was heading back and noticed my grandfather's bull walking toward me. That bull had never paid attention to me any other times I had been fishing, but that day he was looking at me, and that was it. As I was walking back, an uncontrollable fear came over me, and even though the bull wasn't doing anything but watching me fish, I began to run. It was about 100 yards to the fence, and I ran for my life. I looked behind me, and the bull was running towards me, about to catch me. I didn't know it yet, but my grandfather was watching this event unfold and was already racing toward us. The bull got me just as I was about to jump the fence, and within seconds, my grandfather hit that bull right between his eyes with a baseball bat.

I was terrified as my grandfather picked me up off the ground, and you would think I was about to be comforted by his embrace, but I was wrong. My grandfather looked me right in the eyes and said, "Don't you ever let an animal know you are afraid." He told me all animals could sense fear and would take advantage of it if you let them. He told me that his cattle all know he is the boss, and they respect that. I was alright, other than shaken up and dirty from being pushed around on the ground. He told me to go home and see him later. I did as he said, and I came back after lunch.

He came outside and told me he would give me a lesson in fear. He took my hand, and we went right back into that pasture, heading straight toward that bull. We both faced that bull, and then my grandfather let go of my hand to have me stand in front of the bull alone. The bull backed down and walked away. That day I learned a great lesson on how believing a lie can invite trouble into our lives. Even though that bull never had any plans of harming me, I accepted a lie in my head, and the bull acted on it. The bull sensed that and tried to hurt me.

The bull that day is a figure of how satan works. That bull knew my grandaddy had the power to send him to the slaughterhouse and never challenged him. Satan sees the same thing in believers who do not buy into his lies. Like when my focus that day went towards that bull, satan desires our focus to be on him. Our eyes look away from God when we do that, and the enemy has his way with us.

James 4:7 tells us to *"Submit yourselves, then to God. Resist the devil, and he will flee from you."*

When you submit yourself to God, you will not have time to listen to the lies that satan whispers into your ears. It's been a long process for us and will be for you, and I can still on occasions hear the demonic voices speak into my head and that's when I lift my hands in worship and begin to give praise to the mighty name of Jesus. I thank God for the deliverance we experienced here at Springhill

Plantation, and as I focus my attention on God, it silences the demonic voices that were telling me lies.

Chapter Twenty-One
Knowing Who You Are in Christ

Therefore, if anyone is in Christ, he is a new creation; old things have passed away; behold, all things have become new. **2 Corinthians 5:17**

There is a huge difference between believing in God and knowing who you are in Christ. The act of asking God to forgive you of your sins and to become born again is the greatest thing that could ever happen to you, but it should not stop there. God desires much more for you after you ask him to come into your life. I had asked God more than thirty years ago to come into my life, but I had not figured out who was dwelling in me and the incredible power I possessed but was not using.

When I was in high school, there was a bully who tormented me every day. I was terrified of him and let him constantly hit me during the day. He insulted me and took my lunch money. This punishment went on for months, and I just took it. My grades were dropping, and it was all I could think about daily. Gradually my fear of punishment if I got into a fight was surpassed by the pain I was going through.

Teachers were meeting one day, and all the students had to go to the gym while they had the meeting. While I was in school, we were required to dress out in gym shorts and tee shirts, so I was in the locker room. I got my gym clothes on and headed to the main gym area. Just outside the locker room, I ran into him, and as usual, he started bullying me. Anger overcame me, and I beat him into submission in front of the whole school. Blood was all over his face, and he had no answer to my retaliation. The principal discovered what was happening, and nothing was said or done to me. That day I realized that I had something in me that was bigger than what he had in him. I never had another issue with him or anyone since the whole school witnessed the beatdown, and we became good friends after that. What was happening to me at school was physical and mental bullying, and there is no difference in what satan is doing to people today. Discovering the spiritual knowledge of who you are in Christ will cause demons to flee and the mountains in your life to crumble.

In the last battle with the evil spirits, we had in our house, the knowledge of who was in Cindy and I ultimately drove them out for good. I am now keener to my spirit man than I am in my flesh man. There is nothing that I appreciate more than knowing the spirit of the living God is inside of me. If you have given your life to Jesus, you now possess the power to command demons to flee, but only if you know who you have living in you and use that power with authority.

Chapter Twenty-Two
Your Eyes Are the
Window to Your Soul

"The lamp of the body is the eye. If therefore your eye is good, your whole body will be full of light.

Matthew 6:22

William Shakespeare once said, "The eyes are the windows of the soul." That's a perfect revelation for us today from a man born in 1564. I imagine he had to watch what entered his eyes, just as we should be doing ourselves 458 years later. Satan has used these same tactics to lure us into his trap since his great fall from heaven. It was the same trick he used against Adam and Eve in the Garden of Eden when he convinced them to eat from the Tree of Life. Genesis 5:6 says Eve saw that the tree was good for food and was pleasant to the eyes. Do you see what happened? She allowed her eyes to make a life-changing decision even though she knew already that they would surely die if she did.

When reflecting on everything that happened at our plantation, I tried to pinpoint the things that opened the doors to the demons that almost wrecked our lives. One of them was the very thing I have referred to above. We watched many television shows filled with sex, violence, and vulgar language. As we allowed our eyes to see these things, we crept further and further away from any form of morality and let what we entertained ourselves to be of no uplifting value. I allowed myself to watch one show, knowing it was absurdly horrible for me, which caused nightmares for several days. My eyes had opened to something I did not need to see. Has that ever happened to you?

Have you ever gone to the grocery store hungry? How did that work out for you? You went in to grab a few things on your list but came out with three shopping buggies full and a bill of several hundred dollars. Your eyes saw all those beautiful things you could eat and then your mind submitted to its will. It's no different from what you allow your eyes to see and your ears to hear in your daily walk of life. Watching endless hours of cable news shows and listening to the never-ending opinions of people who have no clue of the truth can cause anger to rise in you. I have looked at pornography in the past, and even though it was minimal, it negatively affected me, and my marriage more than I want to admit.

Many top serial killers have claimed they were addicted to porn, like John Wayne Gacy, who murdered 33 young men and boys, and Dennis Rader, the BTK killer from Kansas, who killed ten people, claimed porn influenced them to commit terrible crimes. They all allowed their eyes to open the door to their souls and obeyed its commands when it entered.

Matthew 6:22 says, *"The eye is the lamp of the body; so then if your eye is clear, your whole body will be full of light."* This verse gives us one piece of the puzzle to help stop satan's attacks. What can we do then, with all the visual opportunities that can fill our eyes? One thing you can do is not begin your day with TV or social media but by reading the Word of God. If you fill your spirit with the Word of God, worship, and prayer first, it will set your day to hear the voice of God's spirit. He will gently nudge your spirit when something unclean is about to enter your eyes, and you can adjust to stop it.

In the past, when I got up in the morning, the first thing I did was turn on the news to have my eyes and ears filled with negative things. It was hard at first to stop doing that. Still, I figured out that if you just spent 5 to 10 minutes reading the Bible and then five minutes or so praying, something supernatural will begin to happen in you, and you will begin not to crave what you were filling your eyes with before.

Social media can also negatively influence your life if not controlled. It takes up your whole day before you know it, and all the posts of perfect people with perfect lives can make you depressed. If you knew the truth, that post you just saw of the couple holding hands and kissing while celebrating an anniversary could very well be on the verge of a divorce. Scanning social media and comparing others' relationships with your family and friends is a lie satan can use to cause division between you and others. We are the most connected generation through social media and TV availability but also the loneliest. Maybe it's time to get together physically instead of pressing the like button on each other's posts.

I am not telling you to toss out your TV set or cell phone, as there is nothing wrong with watching a good television show or even keeping up with friends on social media but be aware of the content when you do. Cindy and I have many things we like to see and hear for entertainment, but especially now, after what we experienced are careful about what we allow our eyes to see. I begin my day by reading the Word of God and listening to worship music. Then, when I pray, I ask God to prick my heart if I find myself watching or listening to something harmful to my spirit. Cindy and I can never allow what happened here to repeat itself by opening the door back to the demons God drove out.

Chapter Twenty-Three
Anger

²⁶"Be angry, and do not sin": do not let the sun go down on your wrath, ²⁷nor give place to the devil.

Ephesians 4:26-27

I have heard this scripture my whole life and have not given it much attention. It says not to let the sun go down while you are still angry. If you think about it, that's good advice for everyone. I never thought of myself as an angry man, but that was just my incorrect opinion. The truth of the matter was I was constantly angry, but the enemy had a way of making me believe I was not. When Cindy and I were married, I always had an idea of how good marriage is supposed to be. I would be the man of the house, and everyone else that lived there would obey what I said. For as long as I can remember, I have watched others around me, including some church members treat their wife and families the same way.

As a child, my father gave me very little affection. I am not saying he didn't love me, as I know he did. My father worked long hours and often had to go into the plant seven days a week. He came up very poor and worked tirelessly to ensure we had the things he did not have while growing up.

I emulated that way of life when I married Cindy, and I believe if she knew I was that way, she would not have married me. I never showed affection to her, and there was anger deep in me that I could not explain. This behavior, after many years, caused Cindy and my daughter to build a wall away from me, and when I found myself behind that wall, it made me even angrier. My mind told me that if I was getting up at dawn and working until dark, then they should just love me no matter what.

Do not turn to the right or the left; Remove your foot from evil. **Proverbs 4:27**

After reflecting on this journey of demonic attacks on our lives, I have realized that my anger resulted in more than just a foothold. It caused a wide-open door for all of hell to come into this house, and until I dealt with it, nothing would ever change. **Psalms 37:8** says, *"Refrain from anger and turn from wrath - it leads only to evil."* As you can see from everything you have heard in our story, sin had its way into this house, and my anger was a big part of why it lasted so long.

It was when God opened my eyes to how anger opens doors to the devil, and I began to deal with that part of my life, that another lie from satan was exposed.

I knew I had anger in my heart, but simply knowing that did not make it go away. I asked God to help me in the steps I needed to follow to deal with my anger. The wall between

Cindy and I was huge, and we hardly even spoke to each other most of the time. I could not just tell her that I would not be angry anymore because I knew that was impossible without help. I had no one to turn to, so I began to pray for God to give me the solution.

looking carefully lest anyone fall short of the grace of God; lest any root of bitterness springing up cause trouble, and by this many become defiled;

Hebrews 12:15

Those days there was very little sleep for me, so I would usually lay on the couch at night and replay in my mind how we came to this place in our relationship. One night it was around 1:30 am, and the insomnia was terrible, so I went on to work. I sat in front of the computer and stared at the screen with nothing but sadness. I began to pray for God to show me what I could do to deal with my anger and heal our relationship. Then, in the night's silence, I heard a simple word: Christian counseling. That night I found through my computer a Christian Counseling Ministry. After much prayer and effort, I was able to get Cindy to go with me and began a journey that eventually exposed the core reasons I was angry. It took a long time, but I no longer have that foothold from the devil in my life. My relationship with Cindy and my daughter is now better than ever.

If I hadn't dealt with this anger, I know that the deliverance we received from God could have never happened. Therefore, I thank God every day that He exposed the lies that satan told me concerning anger and go to Christian Counseling.

Chapter Twenty-Four
Do You Unknowingly Worship Idols?

Thou shalt have no other gods before me.
Exodus 20:3 (KJV)

Ask any Christian you want if they worship idols, and they will look at you like you are nuts. The stories in the Bible are everywhere of idol worship and the horrible results from God because of it. Exodus 20:3 says, *"Thou shalt have no other Gods before me."* What does that mean for us today? I have never bowed down to worship an idol, or have I? Modern-day idols are everywhere, and you are probably closer to one now than you believe.

I unknowingly was doing that very thing for years and had no idea. Let's consider what the definition of an idol of today could be. Do you have a statute of some religious god to which you bow down daily? The answer is probably not, and I never did something like that, either. So, what is an idol in your life? Simply, it is anything you value more important than your relationship with God. The list is long of possible idols that have overtaken many Christians lives, and many of them seem, on the surface, harmless.

Around here, the Sunday after a rivalry college football game, many Christians go into depression while the other side is drunk with happiness, depending on what team won. I have always loved college football, and my uncle took me to my first one in 1969. After looking at my heart, I realized that that was one of my idols. I would get physically sick if my team lost, ruining my Sunday and the rest of the week. I did not want to attend church to face those bad Christians who pulled for the other team. I still pull for my team on Saturdays, win or lose, but now I have found that I am part of a team that never fails and that my friend brings absolute joy.

For where you have envy and selfish ambition, there you will find disorder and every evil practice.

James 3:16

One of the biggest idols I realized that was in my life might be surprising to many people. That idol was that I was worshiping myself. It was a practice that I really did not know that I was doing. Do you recall that I mentioned that I do not remember much of my early days as a husband and father? The enemy had a way of perverting my thoughts to believe a lie that my focus on work and then during my off time to do the things I wanted to do for myself was fine.

One of my favorite TV shows has always been *Everybody Loves Raymond.* I am sure many of you probably have seen it or heard of it. The story line is about a guy named Raymond and how he believes the world revolves around him. Everything is fine if He gets his way, and he will do anything to make sure he does. He has a beautiful wife named Debra who works tirelessly to keep the house and raise the children. Raymond in the storylines basically does nothing to help with any chores and believes that since he is being the income provider that was all that is necessary. I remember laughing and telling Cindy that I was sure glad she didn't have a Raymond for a husband. Cindy, I recall, never seemed to respond and usually just kept watching the show. Many times, when Debra had had enough of Raymond, she would call him an idiot. I know now that maybe I was the idiot in our family as I was emulating Raymond to the letter.

Cindy took care of the house and our daughter, and I had very little to do with any of it. My warped mind believed that was that was how the traditional family was supposed to operate. After many years of this practice Cindy had enough and rocked my world one morning on the way to church. I was honestly unaware of what I was doing but realized our marriage was now in big trouble. It took a rude awakening and much work to make the changes I needed but through God and counseling we finally did get our marriage back on track. Satan is doing everything he can to destroy the family unit these days and we was almost one the casualties.

For the love of money is a root of all kinds of evil, for which some have strayed from the faith in their greediness, and pierced themselves through with many sorrows.

1 Timothy 6:10

Money was something that drove me for years, and it was a part of the reason I almost lost my family. My focus was to get as much as possible while unknowingly forgetting the ones I loved the most. Even though making money was my focus, I didn't have much of it. My desire to provide made me selfish with my time. I can genuinely say I do not remember much of my early days of being a husband and father in my pursuit of it. It wasn't that I didn't care about my family, but my total focus was on something else. The more I made, the more I wanted; it seemed like I could never have enough. The curious thing was that the money seemed to disappear as quickly as I made it. While in church, I would hear the scriptures about giving, whether to the poor or the church, and the voices would immediately begin to whisper that God doesn't need any money. After all, I worked hard to earn that income, so why would I hand it over to someone else?

"You have sown much, and bring in little;
You eat, but do not have enough;
You drink, but you are not filled with drink;
You clothe yourselves, but no one is warm;
And he who earns wages,
Earns wages to put into a bag with holes."
Haggai 1:6

Like the other pieces of the puzzle, I learned the absolute truth from God that having a selfish life will make you miserable and even poorer than you already are. The world system says to go after money with all you have, and if you need to step on others to get what you want, do it. The revelation I received from God changed my life and how I think about money. As I listen to the gentle voice of the Holy Spirit when He tells me to give somebody a little money, it is incredible how the money comes back to me but has now increased. The empty feeling of giving away something I worked hard for is no longer with me. God is now my source of income, not my dependence on the world and its selfish system. There is an old saying I will always remember:

"Money is an amplifier; it makes you more of what you already are. Good people do more good. Bad people do more bad."

I had others as well that I had to get under control, such as hunting and fishing, and it was a process that took years. However, there is nothing wrong with any of these things you love to do, as God has given all these things to us to enjoy richly. **Matthew 6:33** says, *"But seek ye first the kingdom of God and his righteousness, and all these things will be added unto you."*

We needed to address all these idols before deliverance could come into our lives and evict the demonic spirits from our houses. Consider searching today and asking the Holy Spirit if there is an unknown idol in your life. If you do, I promise you will hear His gentle voice lead you to what yours is.

Chapter Twenty-Five
Unforgiveness

Then Peter came to Him and said, "Lord, how often shall my brother sin against me, and I forgive him? Up to seven times?" Jesus said to him, "I do not say to you, up to seven times, but up to seventy times seven."

Matthew 18:21-22

Unforgiveness was a massive issue for us in our journey to receive our victory from demonic spirits. We slowly allowed offenses, some small and others more significant, to creep into both our lives. It was something we did not realize was happening, as it was a prolonged process. The things others did to me were genuine and incredibly hurtful, and I had good reason to feel the way I did. Does that sound like something familiar to you as well?

My father was a powerful and sometimes fierce man who demanded respect. He raised us to be the best children we could be, and I will always be thankful for that. As I grew up, we had our good times and not-so-good times, and that story could be one we all could agree with. He focused on providing for us and worked tirelessly to make that happen. Even though I always knew he loved us, he had difficulty showing it, which I struggled with. It took me a long time to realize that his hard work to provide for us was how he showed it. As the years went along, a deep unforgiveness crept into my heart because of that. Even though I felt that way, I never allowed it to be something that caused me never to talk to him again. I respected him and was always there to do anything he asked. On his last day on this earth, I stayed with him because the caregiver could not get there due to an ice storm. It was like he had some beforehand knowledge that he would soon die. He asked for my forgiveness and told me he appreciated me never leaving his side. My heart leaped with joy and love for a man with whom I had a challenging relationship for so long. He died about eight hours later. That powerful message was to let offenses go even if the other person was completely to blame for hurting me.

I remember a sermon from when I was young, and it has stuck with me until this day. The pastor spoke about how when someone hurts us, we tend to point the finger at them and hold unforgiveness. He then pointed his finger at the congregation and showed us his hand. We saw three other fingers on his hand pointing back at him. He said we should look at our own hearts about unforgiveness before we hold it against others. I wish I had remembered that lesson as I grew up, but you can see by what happened to us here that I sadly did not.

The thing about my lesson of forgiving my father was that I had not forgiven Cindy, the one I loved the most. All the years together, we had gone through so much pain, and

I let unforgiveness become a roadblock to any deliverance God could bring into our lives. I knew Cindy felt the same way about me too, as the emotional wall between us was always there. While we were in marriage counseling, that was the main topic for one of the days we were there. You can rebuke satan using the name of Jesus all day long, but if there is real unforgiveness in your heart, I can say from experience that nothing will change. I have a paper stapled to my office wall that communicates:

"TO FORGIVE IS TO SET THE PRISONER FREE AND DISCOVER THE PRISONER WAS YOU"

I heard the senior pastor of the church once say that unforgiveness was like setting yourself on fire and hoping your enemy dies of smoke inhalation. You are only hurting yourself and not the one you choose not to forgive.

In Luke 23:24, Jesus was hanging on the cross in horrible suffering, and you would think that He would be focused on the pain in every inch of His body. He was whipped thirty-nine times, and He dragged His heavy wooden cross up to Calvary to die for our sins. But the hour just before He gave up His spirit, He asked God to forgive them, for they did not know what they were doing. If Jesus could do that while amid all the pain, then can you not forgive that person who has wronged you?

The day the church came to our house to drive the spirits out, if you remember, we were called out by a lady named Paulette before taking communion, saying she knew we had unforgiveness in both of us and we had to deal with it, or nothing was going to change that day. We did, and God moved mightily that day to remove them from our plantation home. If you are having troubles in your life that seem like they will never go away, then do a heart check and ask God to reveal if you have unforgiveness that has not been dealt with.

Chapter Twenty-Six:
Why Did I See and Hear Them?

And when the servant of the man of God arose early and went out, there was an army, surrounding the city with horses and chariots. And his servant said to him, "Alas, my master! What shall we do?" So he answered, "Do not fear, for those who are with us are more than those who are with them." And Elisha prayed, and said, "LORD, I pray, open his eyes that he may see." Then the LORD opened the eyes of the young man, and he saw. And behold, the mountain was full of horses and chariots of fire all around Elisha.

2 Kings 6:15–17

I have prayed to God about why I was allowed to see these demons all these years. After everything that happened, I believe God opened my eyes to see these demons to give others a testimony of His great love and power to deliver us. I am no more special in God's eyes than you, as He loves us all without limits. I have had people ask me whether I actually saw them, and my answer is yes. What started as smells of cigarettes and the sounds of bumps in the night gradually turned into actual appearances. Sometimes it was frightening, and other times it was not. Every time I saw them or heard them, it came with a different emotion. I would get angry and shout at them in Jesus' name, and sometimes fear would take over to have me do nothing. They knew I could see them, like the time "The 1800s Gentleman," as I called him, looked at me when he was standing over Cindy in the barn. When our eyes locked at each other, he instantly faded away.

Our experience with demonic spirits was a long and challenging journey, but it shouldn't have been.

We, like many Christians, did not have our priorities straight with our relationship with Jesus. We had salvation, and heaven was our destiny, but now we know that was just the beginning. We did not understand the power that resided in us, and we allowed satan to become more prominent than God. We believed every lie satan spoke to us, but God opened our eyes to see these things. Step by step, God led us to confront every foothold satan had in our lives. We realized that trying to live victoriously cannot be done alone without other believers walking with you. Unforgiveness will open the gates of hell, and things will not begin to change until you can begin to forgive those who have hurt you, regardless of who was to blame. Allowing anger to go on without ceasing will give satan all he needs to wreck your life, and not knowing who we were in Christ gave satan access to our home without limits. When we eliminated the idols we unknowingly had in our lives and put our focus back on God, there was no more room in our hearts or our house for satan and his demons.

We have not seen or heard of any activity in our plantation home in almost two years. We are no longer afraid of satan or his little demon spirits anymore. It's hard to comprehend, but even our pets know they are gone. While the demonic spirits were here, Zoe and our two cats would never go close to the barn. Now Boo, the kitty, sleeps in the barn, and Zoe runs there daily. We no longer believe the lies and will not listen to his voice telling us we do not have victory in Jesus. We make sure this house is filled with prayer and worship daily, and we also keep a CD player playing worship music twenty-four hours a day. We know our God is a God of deliverance, and we also remind satan daily of that fact.

Chapter Twenty-Seven:
Ghosts or Demons?

"And no wonder, for even Satan disguises himself as an angel of light. Therefore it is not surprising his servants also disguise themselves as servants of righteousness, whose end will correspond to their actions."

2 Corinthians 11:14–15 NET

When word got out that we had purchased Springhill Plantation, hardly a person that came up to us did not fail to ask about our haunted house and the ghosts that dwelled there. When we moved in, the thought of ghosts did cross my mind, and you must admit coming to a house with origins that go back to 1837 does get you thinking. It was intriguing to say the least, but even with that I did not want to believe anything like that was here.

I remember as a young child watching the cartoon *Casper the Friendly Ghost* on television. In the story, Casper was a twelve-year-old boy who died of pneumonia after playing out in the snow for too long. After he died, his father, in his grief, spent the rest of his life trying to find a way to bring his son back. That story for sure tugs at your heart, as any one of us could feel the same way if one of our children were to experience a tragedy like that. It's understandable, as humans to want to believe that there could be a way to have the presence of loved ones with us who have passed away.

The eye of him that hath seen me shall see me no more: thine eyes are upon me, and I am not.

As the cloud is consumed and vanisheth away: so he that goeth down to the grave shall come up no more.

He shall return no more to his house, neither shall his place know him anymore.

Job 7:8–10 KJV

Growing up I was wrongly led to believe the ghosts were simply people who had passed away that had some unfinished business here where they once lived. Maybe they were upset with somebody who had hurt them and now they thought they could come and haunt them to settle the score, or they were here to guide loved ones as they continued life here without them. Modern-day television shows are on every day attempting to convince us that people who once lived can and are with us today. With everything we as humans face every day, such as depression and anxiety, what could be more comforting than to have a loved one who has made it into another world come back to us to make us feel better? If only I had known at the time that ghosts and demons are one and the same.

When my daughter and I both encountered the 1800s Gentleman, he was fully dressed in clothes and looked just like someone you would meet anywhere. My first thoughts were that maybe he lived here in the past, and for some reason unknown to me, I was allowed to see him. Afterall, when we saw him in the barn, he seemed harmless and interested in what Cindy was doing, but when I came home to see him in the office window, that was a completely different experience. I can say the word *friendly* was not what I felt. It was absolute evil that permeated from his presence, and his plans for us were much more than simply getting us to leave this house. If you give it some thought, why would the ghost of a past occupant of this house care if we lived here now, anyway?

During the many years of experience here at the plantation and at our other home when we first married, we both sought answers as to what possibly was going on. Why would friendly ghosts come back and do the things we saw and heard? Why would they fill the house with the smells of cigarette and pipe smoke and open and close doors? What was up with the cold breezes that suddenly passed by me even with the heat on? The biggest question I had was if ghosts were truly kind and harmless, would they come in forms like a six-foot-tall black grim reaper levitating off the floor? My heart knew that these ghosts were a form of a demonic spirit coming to tear our lives apart, and the only place I could get the truth was from the Word of God. It might make your mind feel better to believe in ghosts, but after I saw what they were doing to us, I knew better. Ghosts and demons are one and the same.

There was a certain rich man, which was clothed in purple and fine linen, and fared sumptuously every day:

And there was a certain beggar named Lazarus, which was laid at his gate, full of sores,

And desiring to be fed with the crumbs which fell from the rich man's table: moreover the dogs came and licked his sores.

And it came to pass, that the beggar died, and was carried by the angels into Abraham's bosom: the rich man also died, and was buried;

And in hell he lift up his eyes, being in torments, and seeth Abraham afar off, and Lazarus in his bosom.

And he cried and said, Father Abraham, have mercy on me, and send Lazarus, that he may dip the tip of his finger in water, and cool my tongue; for I am tormented in this flame.

But Abraham said, Son, remember that thou in thy lifetime receivedst thy good things, and likewise Lazarus evil things: but now he is comforted, and thou art tormented.

And beside all this, between us and you there is a great gulf fixed: so that they which would pass from hence to you cannot; neither can they pass to us, that would come from thence.

Then he said, I pray thee therefore, father, that thou wouldest send him to my father's house:

For I have five brethren; that he may testify unto them, lest they also come into this place of torment.

Abraham saith unto him, They have Moses and the prophets; let them hear them.

And he said, Nay, father Abraham: but if one went unto them from the dead, they will repent.

And he said unto him, If they hear not Moses and the prophets, neither will they be persuaded, though one rose from the dead.

Luke 16:19–31 KJV

Notice in verse 26 it says after death there is a great gulf fixed between the believers and the unbelievers and neither can pass from one to the other even if they want to. If you are having experiences like we did in your life, you can rest assured that your ghosts aren't people who departed from this world, but demonic spirits; and they have one thing in mind, and that's to destroy your life.

It may be charming to believe you may have a friendly ghost residing in your house. It sure makes for some interesting table talk among friends. I have had long conversations over the years with some good people who told me they had ghosts, and they not only talked about it, but they seemed thrilled about it. I can imagine how easy of an assignment those evil spirits had there. They were not concerned about being cast out by the name of Jesus, as they were welcomed guests.

Cindy

1. **What did you feel when you saw the plantation home? How did you feel about buying it?** *I thought the plantation home was beautiful. I felt excited and frightened about buying the house.*

   Why were you frightened? *I knew buying a house like this would be a lot of work and responsibility. Also, I knew it would be a fight to get rid of the demons. All old houses have them.*

2. **Did you see anything strange personally?** *I did not see or hear the evil spirits other than the one time in our bedroom when I heard the voice say, "Hey Buddy", but I have felt their presence on many occasions.*

   What was your response to feeling their presence? *I would scream at them to leave in Jesus' name.*

3. **What was your first experience living in the house?** *I felt oppression before we moved in. The house seemed to have a personality of depression. We believed it would pass after we made our home.*

4. **How did your sickness affect your mood? Did you ever feel lonely?** *The sickness made me sad and depressed. I felt lonely all the time.*

Was there anything that you did or that happened to make it easier? *I read the Bible and prayed a lot.*

5. **Was there any time when you felt disappointed in God?** *Many times, I felt disappointed.*
   Was there a specific time that you were disappointed that you could share with the readers? *When I prayed and prayed, but the symptoms and pain would not go away.*

6. **Was there a time you wanted to give up, and if so, how did you gain the strength to continue?** *I wanted to give up many times. However, my strength comes from the Lord; He never gave up on me.*
   Can you share a specific example of how He never gave up on you? *Some days I was so depressed when I woke up in the morning, but I kept my eyes on Jesus, asking for more strength.*

7. **That time you asked Eric to come to the antique store with you, and he kept his distance, was there something that came into your mind that might be the reason he was avoiding you?** *Eric was avoiding me at the antique store because he was mad at me. I don't remember why. He stayed mad at me most of the time. I was not paying much attention to him.*
   How did you process him being mad all the time, and when did you notice a change? *I had learned to ignore him and go on about my day. Eric began to change after we attended marriage counseling.*

8. **What was your impression of the statue?** *I thought the statue was ugly and evil. It made chills go down my spine. When Eric told me to get it out of the house, I jumped up, grabbed it, took it outside to the pasture, poured gas on it, lit it up, and watched it burn with gladness in my heart. I remember having a weird feeling while I watched it.*

9. **What other strange things happened?** *You know how Eric mentioned he found it strange that Zoe and the cats never wanted to go by the barn. The barn always gives me the creeps. While I was feeding the cats, I felt an eerie feeling around me.*
   Has that changed? *I don't feel the evil presence anymore.*

10. **When you were anointing the house for the first time with oil and praying, what was going on in your mind?** *I had mixed emotions the first time we anointed the house and prayed. I thought the evil spirits had to leave. Why do we have to do this? We are Christians whom God was supposed to love and protect. Where was He?*
    How did you answer the question, "Where was God?" *I would cast all my cares unto God. Pray and worship to feel relief.*

11. **Were you surprised that Eric reached out to the church to get help? Why?** *No. I was nervous at first, but after seeing the true love of the church members, I was glad he did.*

12. **The first time Eric asked you to go to the church, why did you say, "Maybe so." What made you say, "Let's try" the second time he asked?** *I had known about that*

church for a long time. It was just another church. I had lost all faith in churches. I also knew we needed to get back to church. We were both spiritually, mentally, and physically empty, dead empty.

13. **How did you feel going back to church for the first time after a long time of not going?** *I felt scared going back for the first time. I was thinking about our past experiences in church.*

14. **How did you feel when a group of church people came over to pray at your house? Did you expect the spirit would be back after that?** *I was anxious about church people coming over to our house to pray. I thought the evil spirits would leave and not come back because we had Jesus on our side.* **What made you anxious?** *Being in this situation for so long, I didn't know what would happen.*

15. **When Paulette asked you if you have unforgiveness toward Eric, you said yes. Are you able to tell us what that unforgiveness was?** *My unforgiveness toward Eric started at the beginning of our marriage. It was a lot of things. He had his brother and friends he went hunting and fishing with a lot. He wasn't interested in spending time with me. He lived with his parents when we were married, and I became his mother instead of his wife. That greatly offended me. He did not know how to be a husband.* **How did you work through that? What do you feel brought about the change?** *I would pray to God to change him and make him a good husband. I felt very happy and relieved when he did start changing.*

16. **How did you feel about that time when you and Eric had to do the warfare by yourselves, which eventually drove them out for good?** *Eric and I did warfare a lot of times. It was intense at that time. We were both drained of all our energy: physically, spiritually, and mentally.*
    How did you restore your energy after engaging in warfare? *We had to pray for God to fill us up again.*

17. **Knowing what you know now, do you think there was anything that you could have done differently?** *We could and should have done things differently. We were walking in the light we had at the time. We were alone in the fight. It wasn't until we were backed by our friends at the local church that we learned about spiritual warfare and the things we were doing wrong: the sin in our lives where many doors were open.*

18. **If there was one thing that you could tell the readers about your deliverance journey, what would it be?** *Don't give up! God is with you even when He feels far, far away. He will pick you up when you fall.*

Naomi

For as long as I can remember, I've been what some people would call "sensitive to the spirit world." For a long time, I chalked my experiences up to my parents' choices of places for us to live. The first home that I remember living in was a small sharecropper's house deep in the country, where my mother's family lived. My dad has told me horror stories of that house, but I don't have any clear or distinct memories of the things that he described. However, the stories still give me an eerie feeling every time they are brought up in conversation. Nevertheless, the series of events that occurred at the Springhill Plantation are something that I will never forget.

A couple years later, I had another experience that I knew wasn't a coincidence. I don't remember exactly when this happened in unison with the other events that took place, but I know it was around the time that my parents began going to a new church that they seemed to really like. We had ordered Chinese takeout and ate in the living room. My parents insisted on watching some boring black-and-white movie, so I scrolled on my phone until they retired upstairs to bed. I remember feeling fine before I fell asleep, only to wake up in a world of misery. When I woke up, it was 3:00 a.m., and I was covered in sweat. My heart was beating fast, and I felt nauseated. I barely made it to the bathroom before I started throwing up what looked like black tar. I knew that it couldn't have been what I had eaten the night before unless I was internally bleeding. I couldn't see clearly, and it felt like the whole house was spinning. I threw up for what seemed like forever. I remember waking up on the bathroom floor soaking wet and confused. So, I wobbled back to the living room and laid down, praying to God that I didn't have some sort of virus sent from hell. Soon after that, I fell back asleep. The next morning, I woke up feeling fine, as if nothing had happened the night before. Was this an attack from whatever demonic entity lurked around in this place?

These aren't the only events that I recall experiencing during the timeframe mentioned in this book. I can recall on more than one occasion when pulling up to or leaving my parents' house, seeing a face in the top floor window of the guest house, or what my dad calls the hospital. This happened at least a handful of times. The face wasn't a distinct one. It was just vague enough to make me feel like I was crazy. For this reason, I didn't mention it until my dad brought up some of the visuals that he had seen. I knew that the guest house was spooky and nowhere I would ever want to spend any of my time., I just couldn't believe that what I thought I saw was real. However, after hearing my dad talk about some of the things that he was experiencing, I knew that I wasn't crazy after all. This entity was real and for some reason, I could see him. Once I realized that, it was enough to make chills crawl up my back.

Last but far from least when speaking about some of the freaky things that I experienced at my parent's house, was the sleep paralysis. If you don't know what I'm talking about, then consider yourself blessed because it isn't pleasant. Imagine that you are groggy and in the midst of falling asleep, and all of a sudden, you can't move. You can see, but barely. But you know deep in your soul that what's happening isn't good. Even though you know that you can't move, something inside you tries really hard, and at this point, you almost feel like you're freefalling. So, you start to panic. And then you wake up, flailing your arms and screaming in desperation.

This is what it was like for me, every time I spent the night at my parents' house. Don't get me wrong, it wasn't the first time I've experienced sleep paralysis, which made it difficult for me to connect it to what was going on. But, just like my dad has always said, "Hindsight is 20/20." And now I know that it was never the coincidence that I thought it was.

Reflections

Have you ever heard the phrase "Hindsight is 20/20"? That expression means it's easier to analyze and evaluate situations when looking back on them in the past than when they were in the present moment. I have done that with this story of our journey with demons living with us in our plantation house. Looking back at every step God took us through, I now realize that if we had not allowed all the footholds, much of the trouble we experienced would not have happened. Do you recall earlier in this book all the times of anointing the house and commanding satan to leave only to have them shortly return? I now know the footholds I told you about allowed them back in. They had to bow to the name of Jesus when we spoke it, but the footholds always invited them to return. If we had taken care of the footholds, there would not have been any reason to do the house cleansing in the first place. All those years, Cindy and I acted on our spiritual knowledge we had at the time, and I praise God that He always meets us right where we are when we call on His name.

Hindsight 20/20 Section

Life is full of decisions and choices that can take us down good or bad roads. Regret is one of the emotions I have dealt with while on this journey here at Springhill Plantation. I imagine everyone can relate to this thought process with life choices they have regretfully made that caused pain for themselves and others. In this section, it would be good to list some of the bad decisions we made and give some of our thoughts on the actions you could take if you find yourselves in a similar situation.

ARE YOU ALONE IN YOUR WALK WITH GOD?

Cindy and I had no fellow Christians to walk with for over six years while the experiences were going on here at our home. Everything changed when God spoke with me to connect to the believers at the local church.

And let us consider one another in order to stir up love and good works.

Hebrews 10:24

Therefore comfort each other and edify one another, just as you also are doing.

1 Thessalonians 5:11

For I long to see you, that I may impart to you some spiritual gift, so that you may be established—that is, that I may be encouraged together with you by the mutual faith both of you and me.

Romans 1:11–12

1. What has been your experience with attending church?

____

____

____

____

2. If you were experiencing demonic spirits as we did, would you feel comfortable enough to tell fellow church members and the pastor? Would you expect them to believe you and not only pray but to act?

____

____

____

____

3. What relationships do you have in place for support and assistance when trouble is happening?

____

____

____

____

4. After you have answered these questions, consider taking these actions.

ACTIONS:

(1) Start searching for a church that will surround you with sound biblical teaching and a congregation that will stand with you if you are in trouble with anything from mental and health issues to issues like we had with demonic spirits.

(2) If you cannot say with certainty that your current church will stand with you on issues like this, then do not let guilt, condemnation, or even friendships stop you from seeking another group of believers to connect with. Trust us that your life could depend on it.

Prayer:

Dear Lord Jesus, I ask You to please guide me to the church that will teach Your Word and worships You with everything they have. I ask you to lead my family and me where You want us to go and not let our worldly feelings get in the way. I thank You, God, for Your guidance today. In Jesus' name, I pray. Amen

WHAT ARE YOU ALLOWING TO ENTER YOUR EYES OR EARS?

"The lamp of the body is the eye. If therefore your eye is good, your whole body will be full of light."

Matthew 6:22

I will set nothing wicked before my eyes;
I hate the work of those who fall away;
It shall not cling to me.

Psalm 101:3

If your right eye causes you to sin, pluck it out and cast it from you; for it is more profitable for you that one of your members perish, than for your whole body to be cast into hell.

Matthew 5:29

1. What kind of television shows do you watch that could be considered dark or maybe even a bit on the sexual side?

____

____

____

____

2. What kind of books or internet browsing habits can reflect the same thing above?

____

____

____

____

3. What type of music do you listen to that may contain graphic language?

ACTIONS:

(1) Take an honest survey of your favorite TV shows and write them down.

(2) Do the same with any books or magazines in your house.

(3) Ask God to reveal anything you watch or listen to that could be a roadblock or foothold.

(4) Consider either blocking or refusing to tune into television shows you know are unsuitable for your spirit.

(5) Find any books or magazines that apply and throw them out.

(6) Continue watching television or reading books you enjoy but filter the content.

Prayer:

Father, in the name of Jesus, I ask You to help me with what I allow into my eyes and ears. Let Your Holy Spirit prick my heart if I watch and listen to anything harmful in my walk with You. Thank You, Lord, for being my filter in this matter. In Jesus' name, Amen!

DO YOU HAVE UNCONTROLLED EMOTIONS?

We were forced to deal with anger, rejection, and resentment toward each other before our deliverance came. These are difficult emotions to deal with, but with God's help they can be overcome.

Let all bitterness, wrath, anger, clamor, and evil speaking be put away from you, with all malice. And be kind to one another, tenderhearted, forgiving one another, even as God in Christ forgave you.

Ephesians 4:31–32

So then, my beloved brethren, let every man be swift to hear, slow to speak, slow to wrath; for the wrath of man does not produce the righteousness of God.

James 1:19–20

Cease from anger, and forsake wrath;
Do not fret—it only causes harm.

For evildoers shall be cut off;
But those who wait on the LORD,
They shall inherit the earth.

Psalms 37:8–9

1. What thoughts of anger or bitterness do you have toward anyone who has hurt you?

____

____

____

____

2. Does it make you mad when someone, especially a loved one, does not agree with you on an essential issue in your life?

____

____

____

____

3. When have you given "the silent treatment" to others when you feel they have wronged you?

____

____

____

____

4. What do you do when someone in your life rejects you?

____

____

____

____

ACTIONS:

(1) Prayerfully ask God to reveal people you have anger and resentment toward and write their names on a piece of paper. Include people who have passed away as well.

Take that paper, pray for each of the names, and ask God to forgive you as you forgive them. Then find a safe place and burn the piece of paper.

(2) If possible, reach out to the people you had on your paper with a kind note or word that you had these feelings and were wrong and ask for their forgiveness. It does not matter if they respond with more harmful words. This action can be a part of what will free you from this foothold that keeps you from receiving your blessing.

(3) Consider reaching out for professional help with a Christian counseling ministry. We did, and it was life changing.

Prayer:
Father, I come to You today to ask for Your help with my emotions. I know only You can change the way I feel towards others. God, I ask You today to soften my heart and guide me to see others as You do. In Jesus' name I pray. Amen

IDOLS

If you recall, at the beginning of this book, I brought a wooden statue from up north on a business trip into my house. I have no way of knowing if that piece of wood had any curse attached to it, but I do know after I brought it in was when our lives began to decline, and we began to see and hear things in our house.

"You shall have no other gods before Me."

Exodus 20:3

"Let your conduct be without covetousness; be content with such things as you have. For He Himself has said, "I will never leave you nor forsake you."

Hebrews 13:5

"No one can serve two masters; for either he will hate the one and love the other, or else he will be loyal to the one and despise the other. You cannot serve God and mammon."

Matthew 6:24

"But seek first the kingdom of God and His righteousness, and all these things shall be added to you."

Matthew 6:33

1. What in your life do you consider more important than God?

____

____

____

____

2. On a Sunday, would you rather do something for yourself, such as play golf, a recreation-type event, or sleep in than attend a church service?

____

____

____

____

3. What is your response when your favorite sports team loses; is it anxiety, anger, or does it ruin your day?

____

____

____

____

4. What in your house could have come from a pagan origin?

____

____

____

____

Based on your answers to any of the above questions, consider the actions below.

ACTIONS:

Pray and ask God to replace the desire to do things for yourself when it's time to attend church and worship Him.

Put God first in your life, and then watch how the things like sports and recreation will become more enjoyable than ever before.

Go through your house and look for anything that could be considered pagan. If you find anything, throw it out or, even better, burn it.

Prayer:

Dear Lord Jesus, I ask You to forgive me for putting anything in my life before You. I want You to be the first place in my life, and I know if I do, you will make everything else I enjoy in life so much better. Amen!

ARE YOU BORN AGAIN?

Soon after we married, when I first saw the demonic spirit in our bedroom, I had been a church member for twenty-four years but never realized I never honestly asked Jesus to come into my heart. I always believed that being a good person and doing good deeds was enough to get to heaven. The whole time I believed that I didn't know I was just eighteen inches away from salvation, as that's about how far it is from your head to your heart. I can say with assurance that if I did not have Jesus in my heart, things would have not ended well here. Consider making Jesus the Lord of your life today and begin a journey that will transform you forever.

Jesus answered and said to him, "Most assuredly, I say to you, unless one is born again, he cannot see the kingdom of God."

John 3:3

. . . that if you confess with your mouth the Lord Jesus and believe in your heart that God has raised Him from the dead, you will be saved. For with the heart one believes unto righteousness, and with the mouth confession is made unto salvation.

Romans 10:9–10

For God so loved the world that He gave His only begotten Son, that whoever believes in Him should not perish but have everlasting life.

John 3:16

1. What does my relationship with Christ look like?

____

____

____

____

2. In what ways have I drawn away from God and let the world be my focus?

____

____

____

____

3. Do I believe being a good person and doing good deeds for others is good enough for me to enter into Heaven when I die? If so, why?

____

____

ACTION:

Take a few minutes and consider your answers to the above questions. If you have not asked Jesus into your heart and you are far away from God, consider making Him your Lord and Savior today.

Prayer:

Dear Lord Jesus, I know I am a sinner, and today I ask for Your forgiveness. I believe You died for my sins and rose from the dead. I turn from my sins and ask You to come into my heart and life. Thank You, Lord Jesus, for saving me this day!

FORGIVENESS

I saved this for the last, as it was our absolute most significant foothold. It allowed demonic spirits to inhabit our plantation and our lives for years. Without freedom from unforgiveness, nothing you will do or can do will stop the forces of hell from wrecking your lives. This one is hard, but this one is huge!

. . . bearing with one another, and forgiving one another, if anyone has a complaint against another; even as Christ forgave you, so you also must do. **Colossians 3:13**

"Judge not, and you shall not be judged. Condemn not, and you shall not be condemned. Forgive, and you will be forgiven." **Luke 6:37**

And be kind to one another, tenderhearted, forgiving one another, even as God in Christ forgave you.

Ephesians 4:32

"For if you forgive men their trespasses, your heavenly Father will also forgive you. But if you do not forgive men their trespasses, neither will your Father forgive your trespasses."

Matthew 6:14–15

Think hard on this one question and answer honestly.

Is there anyone that you hold unforgiveness toward?

- Remember forgiveness does not minimize the offense someone did to you.
- Forgiveness is not forgetting what someone did to you.
- Forgiveness does not require or ask that they forgive you first.
- Forgiveness does not mean that you must reconcile with the person.
- Forgiveness does not have to be for both sides, but only yours.
- Forgiveness is an action that sets you free, not necessarily the other person, as the other person is free to hold unforgiveness against you if they choose.

If you answered yes to the above, consider taking the following actions.

ACTIONS:

(1) Make a list of anyone you hold unforgiveness for.

(2) Reach out to as many as you can and ask for their forgiveness.

(3) Write the names on paper which you cannot reach out to due to death or not knowing where they are anymore.

(4) Now write down your name on that paper so you will be able to forgive yourself as well.

(5) Go to God in prayer and repent from holding unforgiveness to the ones you wrote down and include yourself.

(6) Take the paper to a safe place and burn it as an act of faith.

(7) Praise God for destroying this foothold off your life.

Prayer:
Dear Lord Jesus, I come to You today to ask Your forgiveness. I have held unforgiveness in my heart against others, and today, I repent and turn away from that offense and receive the gift You gave on the cross for my sins. Lord, never let my heart grow hardened against anyone again and

remind me if it starts to. I thank You again for Your precious gift. Amen

HAVE A SERVANT'S HEART

After years of focusing on my problems which, as you have read, were very real and troubling, it was a great revelation that this world did not revolve around me. Watching how other believers surrounded us while we were in the middle of one of the most significant storms, we could ever endure was a game changer. How many people do you know would eat Sunday lunch and then face a house filled with demons? They had a servant's heart and operated in the gift that God gave them. I am not saying that you should do what they did at my plantation home if that's not the gift God has given you. God has a gift He gives to each new believer when they become born again, but we all should have the ministry of serving others. It could be helping a neighbor who is down cut his grass or taking care of a chore for your wife when she has a long day. Maybe go volunteer to help at a homeless shelter. God sees these things and blesses those who do them.

We are a generation that is very focused on ourselves, and we spend significant amounts of time and energy attempting to gather money and accumulate stuff. However, we can watch others suffer from hunger or other issues and turn our heads away, saying they deserve what they are getting. They may very well have caused many of their problems, but I also caused many of the problems here too, and God sent others into our lives to help when there seemed to be no way out. In Mark 15:27, Jesus, near death on the cross, still had a servant's heart while ministering to the thief next to Him after he accepted Him as his savior. In a moment that He should have been thinking of His pain and suffering, Jesus was still thinking of others.

The world's system will attempt to make you believe that if you give your money or time to others in need, you will not have enough for yourself. That's another lie the devil uses because in **Luke 6:38** God says otherwise, *"Give, and it will be given to you: good measure, pressed down, shaken together, and running over will be put into your bosom. For with the same measure that you use, it will be measured back to you."* I can testify that if you give to others in need, God will multiply it back to you. Many people have told me they can't afford to help someone in need or a ministry that helps people on drugs or takes care of the homeless. My answer to them is I cannot afford not to. I watch so many selfish people who work endlessly to make good money but never seem able to get ahead. They wonder why they can't get to that comfortable place where they can have peace. There is no peace in having lots of money, as I would have given everything I had when I had almost lost my wife and daughter due to my selfish and self-serving ways. One of my favorite scriptures concerning money is Haggai 1:6–7:

You have sown much and bring in little, you eat, but you have not enough; you drink, but you are not filled with drink;

You clothe yourselves, but no one is warm, and he who earns wages, earns wages to put into a bag with holes.

My question is, does your bank account seem like a bag full of holes? Verse 7 says to consider your ways. A servant's heart is where you can reach out to those in need and know God is the supplier, not you. You know what you are giving is like a boomerang. That was a toy we played with when I was young. You throw it out, and it comes right back to you, but it returns faster. Most of the time, you will need to get out of its way, and that's how faithful sowing and reaping works. The peace you are looking for is not in gathering more and more worldly things for yourself but in seeing how your generosity, even if it is not much at first, makes a big difference in others' lives. If you have never been a giver, try starting at a fast-food line and paying for the car behind you. The feeling is fantastic, and it doesn't cost very much anyway.

CONCLUSION

Every morning as I have my time in the Word and prayer, I thank God for His deliverance and to never let us forget what He has done to deliver us from these demonic spirits. I also pray to let my spirit man know if unforgiveness or anger is creeping back in. I am not perfect and will never be, so I must be on guard not to go back to my old ways. We know satan is real and desires to steal, kill, and destroy us, and that will never change, but we also know we have the Greater One living in us. **John 10:10** says, *The thief does not come except to steal, and to kill, and to destroy. I have come that they may have life and that they may have it more abundantly."*

We hope our story offers encouragement that no matter what you are going through, there is victory through Jesus. We pray that God opens your eyes to see as well, maybe not to see demons as we did, but to see His power to deliver you from whatever you are going through today. Our heart goes out to everyone who suffers from anxiety and depression. It was something Cindy and I had dealt with for many years, and we, to this day, still must lean on God for help. Our thoughts are also with those who have struggled with marriage issues. In all these areas, satan influenced us with lies and used our lack of spiritual knowledge against us.

Hosea 4:6 says, *"My people are destroyed for lack of knowledge."*

For we do not wrestle against flesh and blood, but against principalities, against powers, against the rulers of the darkness of this age, against spiritual hosts of wickedness in the heavenly places.   **Ephesians 6:12**

There are thousands of books on how to cast out demons and how to do spiritual warfare. They all have great information from the Word of God from wonderful people of God. Messages on spiritual warfare are a topic needed in these last days. Satan is throwing every fiery dart at his disposal, knowing his time is growing shorter. You may not be able to see what we saw, but that makes no difference that he is looking to destroy you and your family. There is no need for fear if you have given your heart to Jesus, as you already have every weapon you need inside you. Satan has no answer to the power of God's Word you possess.

This is not a how-to book but a how-not-to book. Our prayer is that you remember all our mistakes and make adjustments in your life to avoid the hell we brought into our lives.

This house is at peace and so are we. Our marriage that satan sought to destroy is now in a better place than it's ever been. We may have received a few battle wounds, and I know there will be more to come, but now we have something so much greater because we now have a testimony! For the first time in eight years here, we are now living a victorious life. We still have the daily challenges that life here on earth brings us all, but now we have the answer that had eluded us for years. There will be no ghost hunting trips advertised at many plantations around the country here, as there is only one ghost in this house, and His name is the Holy Ghost. Our plantation home has become our refuge instead of the prison it used to be. There is a tangible presence of God walking the halls instead of the demons that used to.

We pray that everyone that reads this book finds the peace of God that we have. It is not easy to live this life, but it is worth it. After going through this, we now know there is a difference between finding happiness and finding joy. Happiness is a temporary event, like when your ball team wins, but true joy in the Lord is never ending regardless of the situation you currently find yourself in. We are reminded of Psalms 23; God walks with us through the valley and doesn't always make the valley go away. Never forget that our God is good and constantly works on our behalf.

The LORD is my shepherd;
I shall not want.
He makes me to lie down in green pastures;
He leads me beside the still waters.
He restores my soul;
He leads me in the paths of righteousness
For His name's sake.

Yea, though I walk through the valley of the shadow of death,
I will fear no evil;
For You are with me;

Your rod and Your staff, they comfort me.
You prepare a table before me in the presence of my enemies;
You anoint my head with oil;
My cup runs over.
Surely goodness and mercy shall follow me
All the days of my life;
And I will dwell in the house of the LORD
Forever.

Psalm 23:1–6

The last word of encouragement we want you to know is if you have believed in God to move with a situation and don't understand why things seem to be not changing, please do not give up. The moment you ask God in faith, He is causing events to happen that you don't even know are going on. He did with us as He gently placed people and events into our paths, leading us through the steps needed for deliverance. He never left us, and He sent His angels to minister and guard us as that process took place.

When our marriage was falling apart, we both could sense that something was happening in the spirit realm and for us to hang on while God made His plans for us known. In the midst of severe anxiety and depression, His gentle voice urged us not to give up, and to hold on to each other and to trust in Him. When all hell was breaking loose around us both and the voices of the demons urged us to give up, there was something deep inside us that continued to resist.

As we reflect now that it's over, it still takes my breath away to look back at what the Lord did for us and His great deliverance that struck like a bolt of lightning here at our plantation and our lives. My heart is full as we come and go at our plantation that once was a place of misery but now has become our refuge.

We pray you never doubt God and His ways as we did. It may have taken years to receive our deliverance, but now that we have it, we see why it did. God had a plan for us the entire time. It was not our plan, but a bigger and better one. I know it sounds unbelievable, but I am thankful to God for allowing us to see and experience the demonic spirits in our home and to hopefully encourage others who feel hopeless just like we did. We pray our story of deliverance after so many years is something you can grab hold of in your situation, knowing God is no respecter of persons. If He did it for us, He will do it for you!

For he has rescued us from the kingdom of darkness and brought us into the kingdom of his dear son

Colossians 1:13

The Springhill House

The Barn

Front view of the hospital.

Cindy and I thank you for taking the time to read our story and experience what God did here at Springhill Plantation. It is easy to gain attention when talking about matters of hauntings and demonic spirits. However, we want the attention to remain on what GOD did and not where He did it. We are excited for the peace we now have and to please understand this is our private residence and we currently are not giving tours. We appreciate you respecting our wishes!

May God richly bless you!

Eric and Cindy Davis